ANIMAL TRACKS
of
Northern California

by Chris Stall

THE MOUNTAINEERS/SEATTLE

To Cathie, Kathryn, Liz, John, Suzanne, Joe, Patty, Tony, Cay, and Lyle.

The Mountaineers: Organized 1906 " . . . to explore, study, preserve, and enjoy the natural beauty of the Northwest."

© 1989 by The Mountaineers
All rights reserved

7 6 5 4 3
5 4 3 2

Published by The Mountaineers
1011 S.W. Klickitat Way, Suite 107, Seattle WA 98134

Published simultaneously in Canada by Douglas & McIntyre, Ltd.,
1615 Venables Street, Vancouver, B.C. V5L 2H1

Manufactured in the United States of America

Book design by Betty Watson
Cover design by Nick Gregoric
Author photo by Angela Staubach
Track on cover: Ringtail

No part of this book may be reproduced in any form, or by any electronic, mechanical, or other means, without permission in writing from the publisher.

Library of Congress Cataloging-in-Publication Data

Stall, Chris.
  Animal tracks of Northern California.

  Includes bibliographical references.
  1. Animal tracks—California. 2. Animal behavior—California. I. Title.
  QL768.S732 1989   599.09794   89-13267
  ISBN 0-89886-195-0

CONTENTS

- 5 PREFACE
- 6 INTRODUCTION
- 11 MAMMALS, REPTILES, AMPHIBIANS, INVERTEBRATES
- 12 Invertebrates
- 14 Deer Mouse
- 16 Dusky Shrew
- 18 Valley Pocket Gopher
- 20 Lodgepole Chipmunk
- 22 Golden-mantled Ground Squirrel
- 24 Pika
- 26 Heermann's Kangaroo Rat
- 28 Short-tailed and Long-tailed Weasels
- 30 Western Toad
- 32 Lizards
- 34 Douglas' Squirrel
- 36 California Ground Squirrel
- 38 Northern Flying Squirrel
- 40 Snakes
- 42 Dusky-footed Woodrat
- 44 Mink
- 46 Western Spotted Skunk
- 48 Mountain Beaver
- 50 Muskrat
- 52 Western Gray Squirrel
- 54 Virginia Opossum
- 56 Yellow-bellied Marmot
- 58 Ringtail
- 60 Marten
- 62 Striped Skunk
- 64 Bullfrog
- 66 Bobcat
- 68 Gray Fox
- 70 Coyote
- 72 Badger
- 74 Fisher
- 76 Porcupine
- 78 Raccoon
- 80 River Otter
- 82 Wolverine
- 84 Pronghorn
- 86 Mule Deer
- 88 Wild Boar
- 90 Bighorn Sheep
- 92 Elk
- 94 Mountain Lion
- 96 Mountain Cottontail
- 98 Black-tailed Jackrabbit
- 100 Snowshoe Hare
- 102 Turtles
- 104 Beaver
- 106 Black Bear
- 109 BIRDS
- 110 Northern Junco
- 112 Killdeer
- 114 American Crow
- 116 Mallard
- 118 Great Horned Owl
- 120 Great Blue Heron
- 122 Golden Eagle
- 124 RECOMMENDED READING
- 125 INDEX

Preface

Most people don't get a chance to observe animals in the wild, with the exceptions of road kills and a few nearly tame species in parks and campgrounds. Many wild animals are nocturnal or scarce, and many are shy and secretive to avoid the attention of predators, or stealthy as they stalk their next meal. In addition, most wild creatures are extremely wary of humans either instinctively or because they've learned through experience to be that way. We may catch fortuitous glimpses now and then, but few of us have the time or motivation required for lengthy journeys into wild country for the sole purpose of locating animals. The result is that areas where we would expect to see animals often seem practically devoid of wildlife.

That's rarely the case, of course. Actually, many animals reside in or pass through all reasonably wild habitats. Though we may not see them, they nevertheless leave indications of their passage. But for the most part such signs are obscure or confusing so that only the most experienced and knowledgeable wilderness travelers notice them.

There's one grand exception: *animal tracks*. Often readily apparent even to the most casual and inexperienced observer, tracks not only indicate the presence of wild animals but can also be matched relatively easily with the animals that made them. I guess that's why I have been fascinated by animal tracks since my childhood in rural New York, and why that focus has continued through two decades of wandering and searching for them in wild lands all across North America.

Animal Tracks of Northern California is a compilation of many years and many miles of my own field work, protracted observations, sketching, photography, and research into a list of articles and books too long to name and too heavy to carry into the backcountry.

Animal tracks may be something you concern yourself with only when you happen on them, or your interest in tracks may become nearly obsessive. You may find yourself hiking with your chin resting securely on your chest, feverishly scanning the ground for clues. You may seek out snow because tracks show up on it better than most other surfaces. In the absence of snow, you might find yourself altering your routes, avoiding bedrock and ground cover, seeking out damp sand, soft dirt and mud along streams, near ponds and lakes, around swamps. You may journey into the desert in early morning, before the sand dries and moves on the wind. After a rainfall, you might make special trips to check fresh mud, even along dirt roads or hiking trails, knowing that among evidence of human activity the animal prints will be clear and precise.

Whatever your degree of interest, I hope you will enjoy using this book, in your backyard or in the wildest and most remote regions of Northern California, and that your interest in identifying tracks grows until you reach the level of knowledge at which you no longer need this book.

Good luck!

Chris Stall
Mulege, Baja California Sur, Mexico

Introduction

HOW TO USE THIS BOOK

1. When you first locate an unknown track, look around the immediate area to locate the clearest imprint (see Tracking Tips below). You can usually find at least one imprint or even a partial print distinct enough for counting toes, noting the shape of the heel pad, determining the presence or absence of claw marks, and so on.

2. Decide what kind of animal is most likely to have made the tracks; then turn to one of the two main sections of this book. The first and largest features mammals; the second, much shorter section is devoted entirely to birds.

3. Measure an individual track, using the ruler printed on the back cover of this book. Tracks of roughly five inches or less are illustrated life-size; those larger than five inches have been reduced as necessary to fit on the pages.

4. Flip quickly through the appropriate section until you find tracks that are about the same *size* as your mystery tracks. The tracks are arranged roughly by size from smallest to largest.

5. Search carefully for the tracks in the size range that, as closely as possible, match the *shape* of the unknown tracks.

6. If you find the right shape but the size depicted in the book is too big, remember that the illustrations represent tracks of an average *adult* animal. Perhaps your specimen was made by a young animal. Search some more: on the ground nearby you might locate the tracks of a parent, which will more closely match the size of the illustration.

7. Read the comments on range, habitat, and behavior, to help confirm the identification.

For the purposes of this book, Northern California is defined as that part of the state lying north of San Luis Obispo, near the coast; Bakersfield, in the San Joaquin Valley; and Barstow, in the Mohave Desert. The area south of that line is covered in the companion volume, *Animal Tracks of Southern California*.

This book is intended to assist you in making field identifications of commonly encountered animal tracks. To keep the book compact, my remarks are limited to each animal's most obvious characteristics. By all means enhance your own knowledge of these track makers. Libraries and book stores are good places to begin learning more about wild animals. Visits to zoos with Northern California wildlife on display can also be worthwhile educational experiences. And there's no substitute for firsthand field study. You've found tracks, now you know what animals to look for. Read my notes on diet, put some bait out, sit quietly downwind with binoculars for a few hours, and see what comes along. Or follow the tracks awhile. Use your imagination and common sense, and you'll be amazed at how much you can learn, and how rewarding the experiences can be.

As you use this book, remember that track identification is an inexact science. The illustrations in this book represent average *adult* tracks on *ideal* surfaces. But many of the tracks you encounter in the wild will be those of smaller-than-average animals, particularly in late spring and early summer. There are also larger-than-average animals, and injured or deformed ones, and animals that act unpredictably. Some creatures walk sideways on occasion. Most vary their gait so that in a single set of tracks, front prints may fall ahead, behind, or beneath the rear. In addition, ground conditions are usually less than ideal in the wild, and animals often dislodge debris, which may further confuse the picture. Use this book as a guide, but anticipate lots of variations.

In attempting to identify tracks, remember that their size can vary greatly depending on the type of ground surface—sand that is loose or firm, wet or dry; a thin layer of mud over hard earth; deep soft mud; various lightly frozen surfaces; firm or loose dirt; dry or moist snow; a dusting of snow or frost over various surfaces; and so on. Note the surface from which the illustrations are taken and interpret what you find in nature accordingly.

You should also be aware that droplets from trees, windblown debris, and the like often leave a variety of marks on the ground that could be mistaken for animal tracks. While studying tracks, look around for and be aware of non-animal factors that might have left "tracks" of their own.

The range notes pertain to California but not elsewhere. Many trackmakers in this book also live elsewhere in North America. Range and habitat remarks are general guidelines because both are subject to change, from variations in both animal and human populations, climatic factors, pollution levels, acts of God, and so forth.

The size, height, and weight listed for each animal are those for average adults. Size refers to length from nose to tip of tail; height, the distance from ground to shoulder.

A few well-known species have been left out of this book: moles and bats, for example, which leave no tracks. Animals that may be common elsewhere but are rare, or occur only in the margins of Northern California, have also been omitted. Some species herein, particularly small rodents and birds, stand as representatives of groups of related species. In such cases the featured species is the one most commonly encountered and widely distributed. Related species, often with similar tracks, are listed in the notes. Where their tracks can be distinguished, guidelines for doing so are provided.

If you encounter an injured animal or an apparently orphaned infant, you may be tempted to take it home and care for it. Do not do so. Instead, report the animal to local authorities, who are better able to care for it. In addition, federal and state laws often strictly control the handling of wild animals. This is always the case with species classified as *rare* or *endangered*. Animals are better left in the wild, and to do otherwise may be illegal.

TRACKING TIPS

At times you'll be lucky enough to find a perfectly clear and precise track that gives you all the information you need to identify the maker with a quick glance through this book. More often the track will be imperfect or fragmented. Following the tracks may lead you to a more readily identifiable print. Or maybe you have the time and inclination to follow an animal whose identity you already know in order to learn more about its habits, characteristics, and behavior.

Here are some tips for improving your tracking skills:

1. If you don't see tracks, look for disturbances—leaves or twigs in unnatural positions, debris or stones that appear to have been moved or turned. Stones become bleached on top over time, so a stone with its darker side up or sideways has recently been dislodged.

2. Push small sticks into the ground to mark individual signs. These will help you keep your bearings and "map out" the animal's general direction of travel.

3. Check immovable objects like trees, logs, and boulders along the route of travel for scratches, scuff marks, or fragments of hair.

4. Look at the ground from different angles, from standing height, from kneeling height and, if possible, from an elevated position in a tree or on a boulder or rise.

5. On very firm surfaces, place your cheek on the ground and observe the surface, first through one eye, then the other, looking for unnatural depressions or disturbances.

6. Study the trail from as many different directions as possible. Trail signs may become obvious as the angle of light between them and your eyes changes, especially if dew, dust, or rain covers some parts of the ground surface.

7. Check for tracks beneath recently disturbed leaves or fallen debris.

8. Try not to focus your attention so narrowly that you lose sight of the larger patterns of the country around you.

9. Keep your bearings. Some animals circle back if they become aware of being followed. If you find yourself following signs in a circular path, try waiting motionless and silent for a while, observing behind you.

10. Look ahead as far as possible as you follow signs. Animals take the paths of least resistance, so look for trails or runways. You may even catch sight of your quarry.

11. Animals are habitual in their movements between burrows, den sites, sources of water and food, temporary shelters, prominent trees, and so on. As you track and look ahead, try to anticipate where the creature might be going.

12. Stalk as you track; move as carefully and quietly as possible.

The secrets to successful tracking are patience and knowledge. Whenever you see an animal leaving tracks, go look at them and note the activity you observed. When you find and identify tracks, make little sketches alongside the book's illustrations, showing cluster patterns, or individual impressions that are different from those drawn. Make notes about what you learn in the wilds and from other readings. Eventually, you will build a body of knowledge from your own experience, and your future attempts at track identification will become easier and more certain.

This book is largely a compilation of the author's personal experiences. Your experiences with certain animals and their tracks may be identical, similar, or quite different. If you notice a discrepancy or find tracks that are not included in this book, carefully note your observations, or even amend the illustrations or text to reflect your own experiences. This book is intended for use in the field as a tool for identifying animal tracks of Northern California.

Mammals
Reptiles
Amphibians
Invertebrates

INVERTEBRATES

The smallest track impressions you are likely to encounter in nature will probably look something like those illustrated at the right.

From left to right, the illustration shows tracks of two common beetles, a centipede, and a cricket. The track of an earthworm crosses from lower left to the upper right corner.

You might initially mistake insect marks for a variety of scuffs and scratches left by windblown or otherwise dislodged debris, the imprint of raindrops that have fallen from overhanging limbs, impressions left by the smallest mice, or even the perplexing calligraphy of toads. If you have more than a square foot or so of ground surface to scrutinize, however, you will usually find that insect tracks form a recognizably connected line; the extremely shallow depth of the trail of imprints is also a good clue that a very lightweight being has passed by.

With literally millions of species out there, trying to identify the insect that made a particular track can be challenging, but there are times when you can follow a trail and find, at the end, either the bug itself, or a burrow which could yield its resident with a little patient and careful excavation on your part. If you spend enough time in one area, you will begin to observe specific species in the act of making their tracks, and that, as with animal tracks in general, goes a long way toward track recognition.

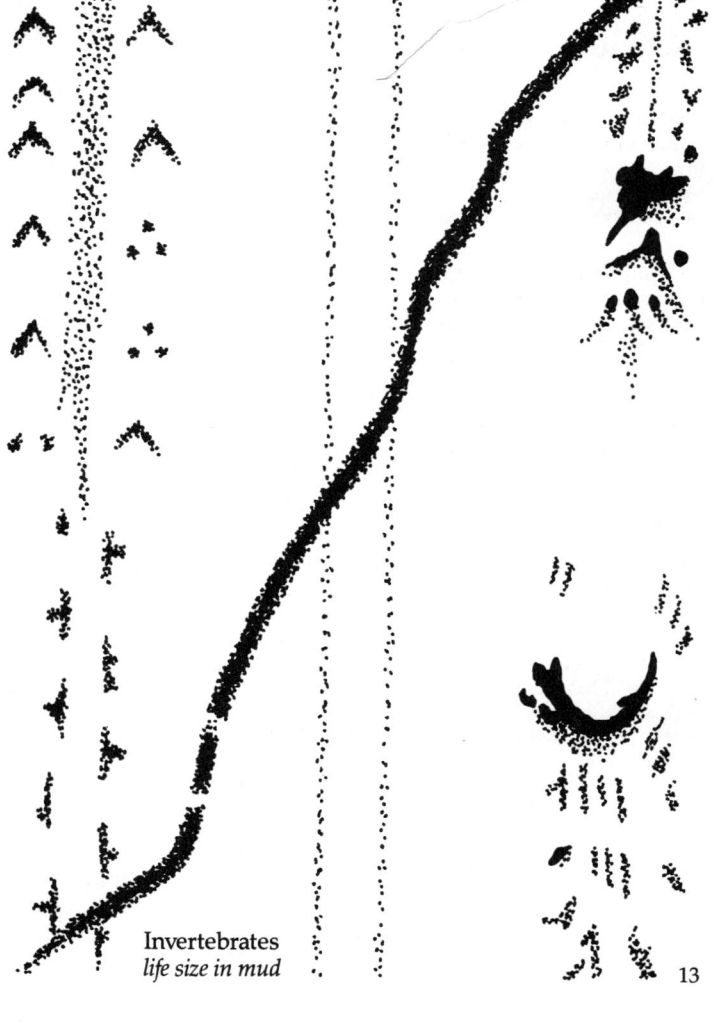

Invertebrates
life size in mud

13

DEER MOUSE *Peromyscus maniculatus*

Order: Rodentia (gnawing mammals). **Family:** Cricetidae (New World rats and mice). **Range and habitat:** common throughout California; in woods, prairies, rocks, and nearly all other dry-land areas. **Size and weight:** 8 inches; 1 ounce. **Diet:** omnivorous, primarily seeds but also mushrooms and other fungi, berries, herbs, insects, larvae, and carrion. **Sounds:** occasional faint chirps, squeaks and chattering.

The abundant, wide-ranging, and familiar deer mouse is a medium-sized long-tailed mouse with pretty white underside, feet, pointy nose, and fairly large ears. Though primarily a mouse of the wilds, it is occasionally found in both abandoned and occupied buildings as well. A good climber, the deer mouse is active year round, generally nocturnal, and adaptable to many habitats. It makes up the main diet of many carnivorous birds and mammals, but is not so completely defenseless, as you might think... it may bite if handled carelessly.

The deer mouse usually leaves a distinctive track pattern—four-print clusters about 1.5 inches wide, walking or leaping up to 9 inches, with the tail dragging occasionally. As with any creature so small, its tracks are distinct only on rare occasions when surface conditions are perfect. More often you find merely clusters of tiny dimples in the mud or snow.

Such tracks could also be made by other "white-footed mice" (e.g., house, cactus, canyon, brush, or pinon mice) or even by other, more distantly related mice (e.g., western, harvest, pocket and grasshopper mice or various meadow mice and voles). Give or take an inch and a few fractions of an ounce, they're all quite similar in appearance. You will need a good pictorial field guide and some patient field work to make positive identifications. Mouse tracks, however, can be distinguished from those of the shrew, whose feet are about the same size: mouse track clusters are wider than those of shrews, and shrews tend to scuttle along or burrow under snow, rather than run and leap. If you follow mouse tracks, more often than not they will lead to evidence of seed eating; shrews are strictly carnivorous.

Deer Mouse
life size in mud

DUSKY SHREW *Sorex obscurus*

Order: Insectivora (insect-eating mammals, including shrews, moles, and bats). **Family:** Soricidae (shrews). **Range and habitat:** throughout mountainous parts of eastern California as far south as Bakersfield; very adaptable; in marshes and fringe areas near water, and in coniferous forests, dry hillsides, and heather. **Size and weight:** 5 inches; 1 ounce. **Diet:** slugs, snails, spiders, insects, and larvae; occasionally mice and carrion. **Sounds:** commonly silent.

Shrews are vole-shaped creatures, but with shorter legs, a slightly more elongated body, and a long pointed snout. Shrew dentists have a big advantage in distinguishing the various species, because variations in unicuspid teeth are all that differentiate many of them. *All* shrews are little eating machines, though, with extremely high metabolism, evidenced by heartbeat and respiration rates around 1200 per minute. In fact, shrews consume more than their own body weight in food on a daily basis.

The shrews' constant and aggressive quest for food makes their tracks, in general, fairly easy to identify. The animals move around with more single-minded purpose than mice or voles, usually in a series of short hops in which the rear feet fall over the tracks of the front feet; the tails often drag, leaving the distinctive pattern shown, usually less than an inch in width. When individual impressions are more distinct, you may notice that shrews have five toes on both fore- and hind feet (most micelike creatures have four toes on the forefeet).

A dozen similar shrew species live around the state, all with similar habits and track patterns. At least the generic shrew *pattern* is unique!

Dusky Shrew
life size in snow

VALLEY POCKET GOPHER *Thomomys bottae*

Order: Rodentia (gnawing mammals). **Family:** Geomyidae (pocket gophers). **Range and habitat:** throughout California; fields, pastures, grasslands, and roadsides. **Size and weight:** 9 inches; 6 ounces. **Diet:** various foliage, twigs, bark, roots and tubers. **Sounds:** silent.

Pocket gophers are peculiar, highly evolved burrowing rodents named for the fur-lined cheek pockets in which they carry both food and nesting materials; the pockets can be turned inside out to empty their contents and for cleaning.

Pocket gophers look like small buff to grayish rats except that their large, yellowish front teeth are always showing; their lips close behind the teeth, so the animals can gnaw through earth and roots during tunneling without getting dirt in their mouths. Pocket gophers spend most of their lives in extensive tunnel systems. The Sierra pocket gopher spends winters above ground, tunneling in the snow. In spring it cleans out its underground tunnel system, pushing accumulated soil into the snow tunnels. When the snow melts, meandering cores of this packed soil thus mark the courses of the winter tunnels. Other signs of pocket-gopher activity include tracks or tooth marks on limbs near their tunnel entrances, and plugged earthen mounds near those entrances. Other California pocket-gopher species include the northern, Mazama, and Townsend pocket gophers, all from the northern margins of the state.

The tracks are similar in size to those of a chipmunk, but the pocket gopher's elongated heel pads leave larger impressions. The most distinctive characteristic of pocket-gopher tracks, however, is the imprint of the five toes on both front and rear feet; the relatively long digging claws on its front feet leave prominent marks, and the distance between the toe and the claw marks is greater than with any other similar-sized creature.

Valley Pocket Gopher
life size in mud

LODGEPOLE CHIPMUNK *Eutamias speciosus*

Order: Rodentia (gnawing mammals). **Family:** Sciuridae (squirrels). **Range and habitat:** most of central and eastern California; from low sagebrush deserts and rocky areas with scattered trees to coniferous and mixed forests and adjacent chaparral at all altitudes, common in parks and camping areas. **Size and weight:** 9 inches; 2 ounces. **Diet:** vegetation, berries, grains, seeds, insects, and carrion. **Sounds:** shrill and persistent "chip, chip."

The most widespread chipmunk species in California, the lodgepole chipmunk is difficult to distinguish from several other locally common chipmunks, including the least, Allen's yellow-pine, Merriam's, alpine, Sonoma, Panamint, long-eared, and several others. All have more or less distinctive black and white stripes from nose to their moderately bushy tail, and they chatter nearly constantly as they leap and scurry over the ground and up and down tree trunks during the daylight hours.

The track patterns of chipmunks are roughly 2 inches in width, with 7 to 15 inches between clusters of prints. Chipmunks often run up on their toes, so rear-heel imprints may not show at all or may be less clear. The hind-foot tracks (five-toed) almost always fall closer together than and in front of the forefoot tracks (four-toed), typical of all squirrel-family members. If you find tracks like these in midwinter, however, you can assume they were left by a small squirrel rather than a chipmunk, because chipmunks tend to hole up with food caches in winter. If they are indeed chipmunk tracks, you will probably catch sight of the maker, because chipmunks are noisy and not all that timid, particularly in campgrounds; in fact, they will more than likely approach you for a handout.

Lodgepole Chipmunk
life size in mud

GOLDEN-MANTLED GROUND SQUIRREL
Copperhead, flickertail

Spermophilus lateralis

Order: Rodentia (gnawing mammals). **Family:** Sciuridae (squirrels). **Range and habitat:** mountainous areas of northern and eastern California; in chaparral and in semiopen coniferous forests to and above timberline. **Size and weight:** 12 inches; 9 ounces. **Diet:** omnivorous, including herbs, seeds, fruits, insects, eggs, and carrion. **Sounds:** usually silent; shrill and rapid chirps signal alarm.

The ground squirrels of California vary greatly in appearance and habits, but they all are *terrestrial*, living in extensive burrow systems. They tend to stand up and whistle or trill when alarmed, rather than chattering like their arboreal cousins. Some are solitary, others colonial. Most hibernate 7 or 8 months of the year, but even when active rarely venture far from their burrows.

The golden-mantled is a wide-ranging and very attractive mountain ground squirrel, with the lateral black and white body stripes of a chipmunk, but a good deal larger and without facial stripes. Other ground squirrels in the state tend to be gray, faintly speckled, and about the same size, except for the California ground squirrel, which is almost the size of a western gray squirrel.

The track shape and pattern of the golden-mantled ground squirrel is common to most ground squirrels. The truncated inner toe of the front foot may leave only a slight or no imprint. Nine to 18 inches separate groups of four prints made by running animals; they usually walk only at den entrances. Ground squirrels tend to be more flat-footed than tree squirrels, and whereas tree squirrel tracks are never far from trees and usually lead to or away from them, ground squirrel tracks always lead to or from the squirrels' subterranean homes. The toes, adapted for digging, tend to leave splayed prints; and the claws often leave imprints farther from the toes. A final clue: ground squirrels almost never leave tracks in snow; they are too busy sleeping away the winter.

Golden-mantled Ground Squirrel
life size in mud

PIKA
Cony
Ochotona princeps

Order: Lagomorpha (rabbitlike mammals). **Family:** Ochotonidae (pikas). **Range and habitat:** northern and central Sierra; in scree slopes and rock slides, usually from 6000 feet above sea level up to timberline. **Size and weight:** 8 inches; 6 ounces. **Diet:** grasses, and herbaceous vegetation. **Sounds:** series of short squeaks, warning of danger.

In scree slopes along the Tioga Pass highway in Yosemite National Park, travelers often see chipmunks, ground squirrels, and pikas together, but there's no mistaking pikas, little grayish-brown furballs with short round ears and no tail showing, usually sitting quietly in the sun on a promontory or moving quite fluidly over the rocky shards. Pikas spend their summers making little haystacks of clipped vegetation that dry in the sun among the rocks. The hay serves as food supplies for the winter, when the pika remains active but often stays below the snow surface. Its peculiar call is also distinctive and might puzzle you when you hear it coming up from beneath a deep snow cover.

Pika tracks are not easy to locate because this small relative of rabbits and hares lives primarily among rocks and—in winter—beneath snow surfaces, but occasionally you will find them on early-fall or late-spring snow, or in mud around alpine ponds near the animal's stony home. The pika's hairy feet and toes—five front and four rear—and shuffling gait produce what looks like miniature bear tracks; its running trails are composed of clusters not more than 3 inches wide and usually about 10 inches apart.

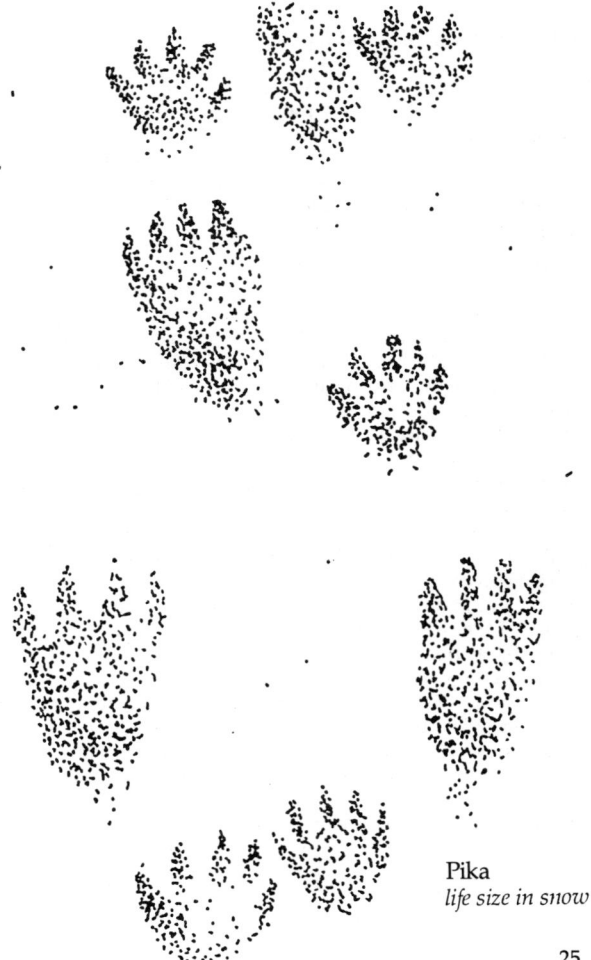

Pika
life size in snow

25

HEERMANN'S KANGAROO RAT *Dipodomys heermanni*

Order: Rodentia (gnawing mammals). **Family:** Heteromyidae (kangaroo mice and rats). **Range and habitat:** most of western and central California, except absent from much of San Joaquin and Sacramento Valleys; on dry grassy plains and open, brushy foothills, preferring gravelly ground. **Size and weight:** 11 inches, much of which is tail; 2.5 ounces. **Diet:** seeds and great variety of vegetation. **Sounds:** thumps feet when alarmed.

At least 10 kangaroo rat species can be found in various parts of the state. Heermann's is a widespread, medium-sized rat whose characteristics are representative of the lot: a chubby rat with buff or gray fur, white belly and feet, white stripes across the outer thigh meeting at the base of the tail, strong hind legs with oversized rear feet, and a very long, bushy-tipped tail. It is nocturnal, prefers arid or semiarid habitats, and lives in extensive burrow systems, which are often—especially in sandy areas—as much as 3 feet high and 12 feet or so in diameter, with many entrance holes. Around these burrows, and along the paths connecting them to feeding places or other mounds, you will often find cut plant fragments. Kangaroo rats rarely travel more than about 50 feet from these not inconspicuous nests.

There is great size variation among California's kangaroo rats, ranging from Merriam's, which measures about 9 inches from nose to tail, to the desert kangaroo rat, whose tail alone may be that long. Some species have 4 toes on their hind feet, some have 5. All have the same basic track pattern. When a kangaroo rat moves slowly, as while feeding, most of its 1.5–2-inch hindprints are visible, as are impressions of the smaller forepaws and the long tail. At speed, however, when the animal is making leaps of 3 to 9 feet, only the rear toes contact the ground. Combined with other signs, the resulting, widely spaced pairs of prints clearly indicate the passage of these interesting rodents. Similar, but smaller, more closely spaced tracks are made by pocket and kangaroo mice.

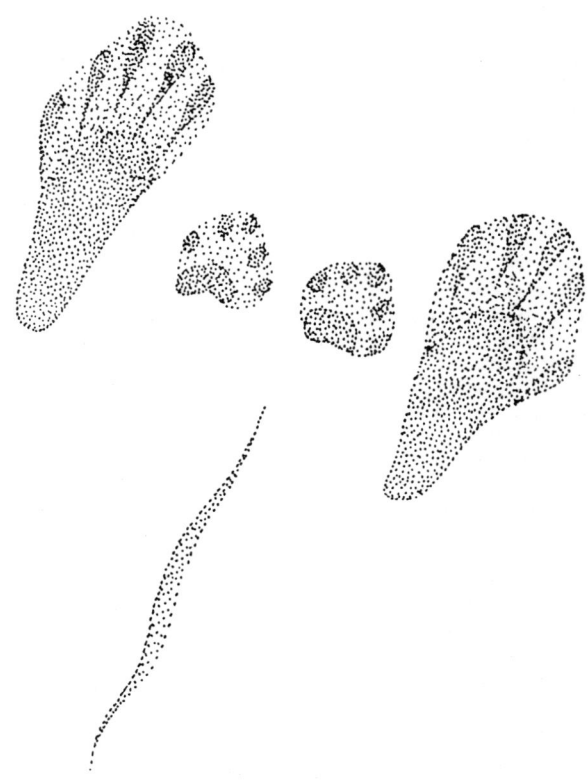

Heermann's Kangaroo Rat
life size in sand

SHORT-TAILED WEASEL — *Mustela erminea*
LONG-TAILED WEASEL — *Mustela frenata*

Order: Carnivora (flesh-eating mammals). **Family:** Mustelidae (the weasel family). **Range and habitat:** short-tailed—northern third of the state except Sacramento Valley area; long-tailed—throughout the state except the desert areas; in varied grasslands, wetlands, farmlands, and brushy or wooded terrain to above timberline; usually near water. **Size and weight:** short-tailed—12 inches; 6 ounces; long-tailed—14 inches, 10 ounces. **Diet:** rodents, including chipmunks, ground squirrels, and mice; occasionally moles. **Sounds:** generally silent; occasionally squeals.

The short-tailed weasel is an inquisitive and aggressive little carnivore with a thin, elongated body and short, bushy tail. Brown with a white underside and feet during the summer months, in winter the weasel turns almost entirely white, save for the tip of its tail, which remains black. In this fur the short-tailed weasel is commonly known as an ermine.

The long-tailed weasel is a slightly larger and longer-tailed version of the short-tailed weasel. It, too, is an aggressive hunter by day and night, will climb and swim but generally confines its activities to an agile pursuit of prey on the ground, where it also finds various burrows, and it, too, grows a white coat with black tail tip in winter.

Short-tailed and long-tailed weasel tracks are impossible to distinguish conclusively. Generally, short-tailed track clusters are about 2 inches wide and less than 3 feet apart, whereas long-tailed weasel clusters may be as much as 3 inches in width, with leaps of up to 50 inches. But how do you really know whether the tracks were made by a large short-tailed weasel or a small long-tailed weasel?

If close study doesn't reveal fifth toe prints, individual weasel tracks can be tough to distinguish from those of squirrels or rabbits. But weasels usually *alternate* long and short bounds, and leave lines of doubled-over tracks with occasional tail-drag marks, whereas rabbits and squirrels tend to leave four separate prints in each cluster without tail drags. The latter also leave evidence of vegetarian diets, whereas weasels, being carnivores, do not.

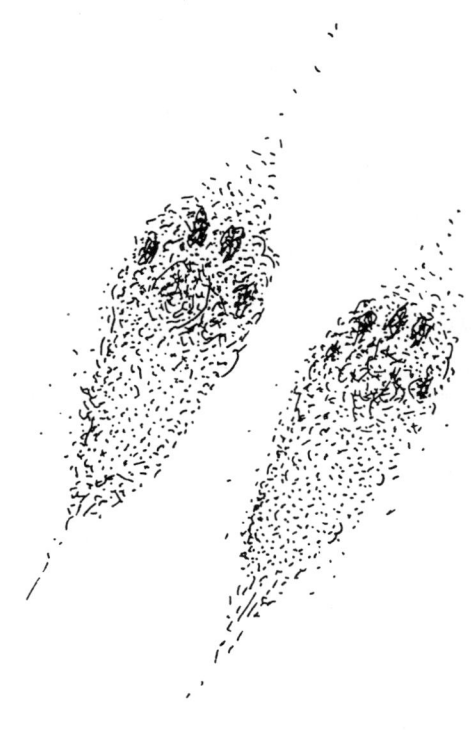

Short-tailed Weasel
life size in snow

WESTERN TOAD *Bufo boreas*

Order: Salientia (frogs, toads, and allies). **Family:** Bufonidae (true toads). **Range and habitat:** widespread throughout California; in moist woodlands and adjoining areas, wherever insects are abundant, usually but not necessarily within a mile of permanent dampness. **Size and weight:** 4 inches; 2 ounces. **Diet:** insects. **Sounds:** high-pitched musical trills.

Toads are small, froglike animals with dry, warty skin, in a variety of reddish, brown, and gray colors. They are primarily nocturnal, but can be seen at dawn or dusk, or even by day, crouching in a little niche, waiting for bugs.

Unlike frogs, toads often travel fairly far from sources of water. In fact, red-spotted toads inhabit much of the arid region of southeastern California, receiving moisture only through diet for most of the year. They do require water for breeding, however; look for their long, ropy strings of eggs in stagnant pond water.

Individual toad tracks can be confusing and might be mistaken for the tiny dimples and scratchings of tracks left by small mice or insects. A toad tends to sit quietly waiting for insects to fly past it, at which time it takes a few leaps in the direction of the wing noise, snares the bug with its long, sticky tongue, then repeats the procedure. Thus it may change direction of travel abruptly and often, commonly backtracking over earlier prints, which makes a very confusing picture on the ground.

Toad tracks generally consist of nothing more distinct than a trail of little holes and scrapes, with impressions that sometimes resemble little toad hands. The distinguishing characteristics are the mode of wandering, the short rows of four or five round dimples left by the toes of the larger rear feet, and the drag marks often left by the feet as the toad moves forward; those toe-drag marks point in the direction of travel.

You won't get warts from handling toads, but make sure you don't have insect repellent or other caustic substances on your hands that might injure the toad's sensitive skin.

Western Toad
life size in mud

31

LIZARDS
Order: Squamata

Lizards are the largest group of living reptiles worldwide, with 115 species in North America alone. Lizards exist in a bewildering array of sizes, colors, and shapes, from tiny geckos less than 3 inches long to the Komodo dragons of Indonesia, some of which are close to 10 feet from nose to tip of tail. Numerous lizard species reside in California, particularly in the desert region.

Although pinning down which species made a particular track may prove difficult or impossible, you should find it fairly easy to recognize that the trail was left by a lizard of some sort. Portions of the low-slung belly and tail usually drag along the surface it's walking on, and the five-toed feet alternate, rather than fall side by side, distinguishing the tracks from those left by small mammals. At times, the waving tail may brush away some details of the footprints. Turtles sometimes leave similar trails, but a turtle with the same size feet as a lizard would usually leave a wider trail.

The straddle and gait of lizards vary widely depending on their size, of course; the illustration represents a lizard of about 8 inches, nose to tail tip.

Lizard
life size in sand

DOUGLAS' SQUIRREL
Chickaree

Tamiasciurus douglasii

Order: Rodentia (gnawing mammals). **Family:** Sciuridae (squirrels). **Range and habitat:** northern and eastern California, south through Sierra Nevada; in coniferous or mixed forests and occasionally nearby on swamp fringes. **Size and weight:** 10 inches; 7 ounces. **Diet:** nuts, fungi, insects, larvae, cones, seeds, and vegetation. **Sounds:** a great variety of noisy, ratchetlike sounds.

Douglas' squirrel is active during the day year round. Quite common throughout most of its range, this small, noisy squirrel is easy to identify by its rust or grayish-red coat of fur, fluffy rust-colored tail, and the white rings around its eyes. It lives in ground burrows as well as in downed logs and standing trees and is particularly fond of pine cones, which it shucks for the seeds, leaving piles of cone remnants everywhere. Occasionally in the fall, you may be startled by green cones falling systematically and seemingly unaided from tall coniferous trees. Douglas' squirrel is up there, out of sight, cutting the cones; later it will gather them from the forest floor and hide them away for the cold months to come.

The Douglas' squirrel has long, curved toenails that act as hooks for tree climbing and which often leave definite imprints. Clear tracks show the squirrel's four toes on its front feet, and the five toes on its hind feet, which usually fall ahead of the front. Often the heel marks will be absent because the red squirrel is usually running quickly and nervously when it is on the ground; the track spacing may vary widely, with leaps from 8 to 30 inches. Individual prints may be as long as 1.5 inches.

Douglas' Squirrel
life size in mud

CALIFORNIA GROUND SQUIRREL *Spermophilus beecheyi*

Order: Rodentia (gnawing mammals). **Family:** Sciuridae (squirrels). **Range and habitat:** throughout northern California; in nearly all open areas, avoids thick chaparral and dense forest. **Size and weight:** 17 inches; 1.5 pounds. **Diet:** omnivorous including green vegetation, seeds, acorns, mushrooms, fruit, berries, birds, eggs, insects. **Sounds:** loud chirp when alarmed.

Common, widespread, and active by day, the California ground squirrel is often seen and easy to recognize. The largest ground squirrel in the state, it looks like a very fat western gray squirrel with only a slightly fluffy tail. Its coat is pale brownish gray, with lightly speckled back and rump. Its gray tail is fringed in white, and across the top of its shoulders, there is a V of darker fur that points forward. The California ground squirrel lives in a complex of burrows sometimes 200 feet or more in length, on gentle slopes around the state, rarely venturing far from the interconnected system of runways between its entrance mounds.

Although the squirrel may climb into a bush to bask in the early morning sun, it normally stays on the ground. It lives in loose colonies, with 4 or 5 adults sharing an acre or so of space. Throughout most of the state, the California ground squirrel spends the hot months of summer and early fall asleep in its nest below ground. At higher elevations, it may reverse the pattern.

Regrettably, the California ground squirrel does significant damage to crops and pastureland, and its fleas often carry plague.

California ground squirrel tracks are easy to identify. For one thing, no other large squirrel shares the open, grassy habitat of this species. The track pattern is characteristic of the squirrel family, usually a cluster of 4 prints less than 3 inches wide, with the front footprints closer together and slightly behind those left by the rear feet. These ground squirrels have 5 toes on both front and rear feet, but the front thumbs are so truncated that they often do not leave marks. Front toe imprints tend to be slightly lopsided or offset toward the outside of the line of travel. Walking stride is about 2 inches, with leaps of 10–18 inches.

California Ground Squirrel
life size in sand

NORTHERN FLYING SQUIRREL *Glaucomys sabrinus*

Order: Rodentia (gnawing mammals). **Family:** Sciuridae (squirrels). **Range and habitat:** portions of northern and eastern California south to the mountains near Palm Springs; in coniferous and, occasionally, mixed forests at higher altitudes. **Size and weight:** 11 inches; 6 ounces. **Diet:** bark, fungi, lichen, seeds, insects, eggs, and carrion. **Sounds:** generally silent; occasionally makes chirpy, birdlike noises.

Northern flying squirrels are nocturnal, so chances are you will only see their tracks, unless you happen to knock against or cut down one of the hollow trees in which they are fond of nesting; in that case, if the squirrel that runs out is gray, you've had a rare glimpse of the northern flying squirrel.

During summer, the northern flying squirrel doesn't leave much evidence of its passage. It lives mostly in trees, using the fur-covered membrane that extends along each side of its body from the front to the rear legs to glide between trees and occasionally from tree to earth, where it usually leaves no marks on the ground cover of its forest habitat. On snow-covered surfaces, however, its tracks can be identified because they lead away from what looks like a miniature, scuffed snow-angel, the pattern left when the squirrel lands at the end of an aerial descent. The tracks may wander around a bit if the squirrel has foraged for morsels, but they will lead back to the trunk of a nearby tree before long.

Northern Flying Squirrel
life size in snow

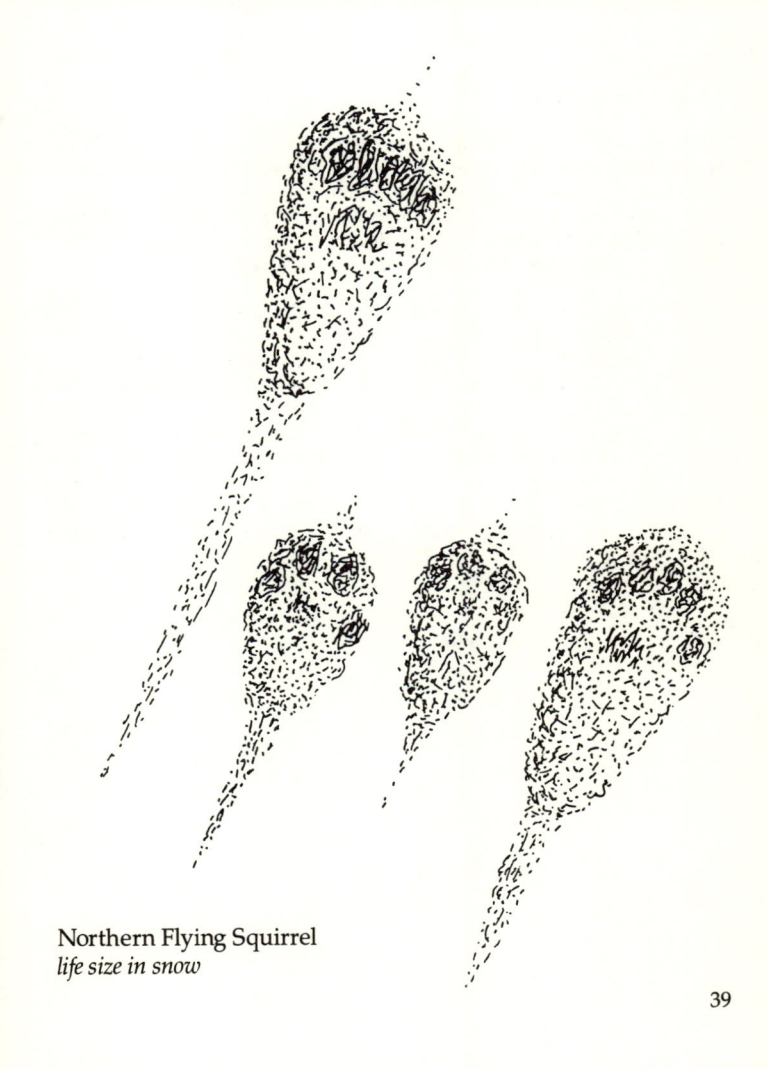

SNAKES
Order: Squamata

There are 115 species of snakes living in North America, 19 of which are poisonous. They vary in length from 6 inches to nearly 9 feet. Many species of snakes in a variety of sizes and colors live all over California in nearly every imaginable habitat. Many poisonous snakes also inhabit parts of the state, including five species of rattlesnakes in southeast California, and the western rattlesnake elsewhere.

Snake tracks are easy to recognize, and the width of the snake is pretty easy to guess. It's usually difficult to tell a snake's direction of travel from its trail over flat ground, because snakes don't usually move fast enough to dislodge peripheral debris. If you can follow the trail far enough, however, you may find a place where the elevation or type of ground surface changes; there, with careful investigation, you might find some minute clues about the direction of travel.

It is likewise difficult to identify a snake by tracks, except for the sidewinder, one of the rattlesnakes of southeastern California, which leaves a trail of parallel J-shaped marks behind it as it flips its body repeatedly along the ground of its arid, sandy habitat.

Snake
life size in sand

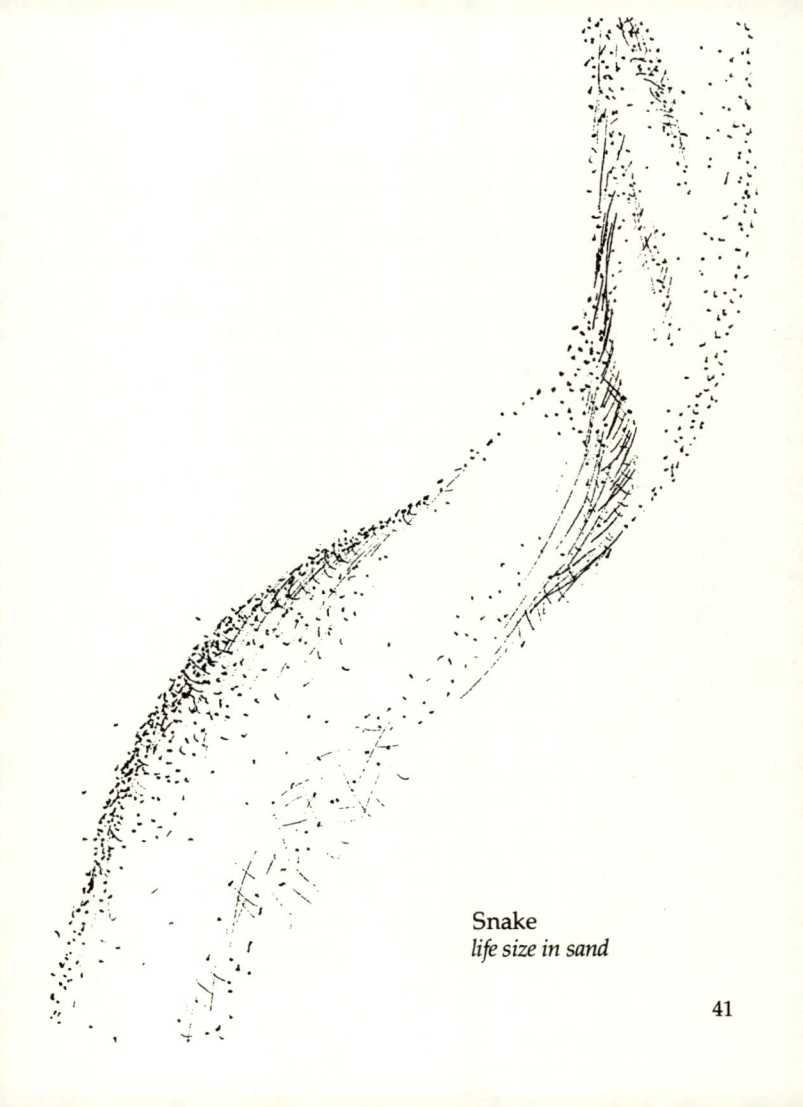

DUSKY-FOOTED WOODRAT *Neotoma fuscipes*
Pack rat, trade rat

Order: Rodentia (gnawing mammals). **Family:** Cricetidae (New World rats and mice). **Range and habitat:** widespread throughout all of western and most of central California, absent from central Sacramento and San Joaquin valleys; in coniferous forests, cliffs, caves, rocky areas at all elevations, and occasionally in abandoned buildings; avoids deserts. **Size and weight:** 15 inches; 20 ounces. **Diet:** vegetarian, supplemented with insects, eggs, carrion when available. **Sounds:** occasionally drums and thumps feet.

This native American rat is active year round but it is seldom sighted in the wild, as it is generally nocturnal. The dusky-footed woodrat is slightly larger than the imported Norway and black rats and has a furry, not scaly, tail. Woodrats avoid human habitations, although they may "borrow" shiny objects from campsites.

The dusky-footed woodrat is a skilled and frequent climber and often builds large nests of sticks in trees. It also places its compartmentalized "lodges" in clumps of brush or on the ground.

Three species are present in California. The dusky-footed is the mid-sized model of brushlands; the desert woodrat is slightly smaller, inhabiting the desert floors and rocky slopes of the southern half of the state; the bushy-tailed woodrat, slightly larger, lives among the high mountain cliffs and rockslides of the north and east. All are pale grayish brown, rat-like in appearance, the bushy-tailed woodrat having a tail with longer hair than the others.

Woodrats have fairly stubby toes, four on the fore feet and five on the hind, that usually leave uniquely shaped tracks with no claw marks. The tracks are roughly in line when walking and grouped as illustrated when running, with 8 or more inches separating the clusters of prints. Like most small rodents, when woodrats leap, their front feet land first, followed by the back feet which come down ahead of the front imprints, providing the spring into the next leap. If the characteristic stubby-toed imprints are not clear, the short spacing relative to foot size should help distinguish woodrat tracks from similar ones made by other animals of comparable size.

Dusky-footed Woodrat
life size in mud

MINK
Mustela vison

Order: Carnivora (flesh-eating mammals). **Family:** Mustelidae (the weasel family). **Range:** northern California southward in the Central Valley to Sacramento and throughout the Sierra Nevada; in brushy or open forested areas along streams, lakes, and other wetlands. **Size and weight:** 24 inches; 3 pounds. **Diet:** primarily muskrats and smaller mammals; also birds, frogs, fish, crayfish, and eggs. **Sounds:** snarls, squeals, and hisses.

About the size of a small cat and medium brown all over, the mink is an excellent swimmer and may wander several miles a day searching for food along stream- and riverbanks and around the shorelines of lakes. Its den, too, is usually in a stream- or riverbank, an abandoned muskrat nest, or otherwise near water. Generally a nocturnal hunter, its tracks are likely to be the only indication you have of its presence.

The mink leaves either groups of four tracks like those illustrated or the characteristic double pair of tracks, usually not more than 26 inches apart. The tracks nearly always run along the edge of water. Though it has five toes both front and rear, it is quite common for only four-toed imprints to be apparent. Like all mustelids, the mink employs its scent glands to mark territory; so, as you track it through its hunting ranges, you may notice a strong scent here and there, different but as potent as that of its relative the skunk. You might also, in snow, find signs of prey being dragged, invariably leading to the animal's den.

Mink
life size in mud

WESTERN SPOTTED SKUNK
Civet cat, hydrophobia cat

Spilogale gracilis

Order: Carnivora (flesh-eating mammals). **Family:** Mustelidae (the weasel family). **Range and habitat:** widespread throughout California; in brushy or sparsely wooded areas along streams, among boulders, and in prairies. **Size and weight:** 25 inches; 3 pounds. **Diet:** omnivorous, including rats, mice, birds, insects, eggs, carrion, seeds, fruit, and occasionally vegetation. **Sounds:** usually silent.

The spotted skunk is the smallest and most visually interesting of the North American skunks. About the size of a small housecat, with an assortment of white spots and streaks over its black coat, the spotted skunk has finer, silkier fur than the other skunks, is quicker and more agile, and occasionally climbs trees, although it doesn't stay aloft for long. Like all skunks, it is primarily nocturnal, but you might see it at dawn or dusk, or foraging during the daylight in winter, when hunger keeps it active. Skunks have the most highly effective scent glands of all the mustelids and can, when severely provoked, shoot a fine spray of extremely irritating methyl mercaptan as far as 25 feet. Everyone knows what that smells like.

Skunk tracks are all similar, with five toes on each foot leaving prints, toenail prints commonly visible, and front tracks slightly less flat-footed than rear. Only size and irregular stride may help distinguish the tracks of the spotted skunk from those of the twice-as-large striped skunk. Spotted skunk tracks will be about 1.25 inches long at most; adult striped skunks leave tracks up to 2 inches in length. On the other hand, the quick spotted skunk leaves a foot or more between *clusters* of prints when running, while the larger striped skunk lopes along with only about 5 or 6 inches between more strung-out track groups.

Because skunks can hold most land animals at bay with their formidable scent, owls are their chief predators. If you are following a skunk trail that ends suddenly, perhaps a bit of black and white fur remaining mysteriously where the tracks disappear, you might be able to guess what transpired.

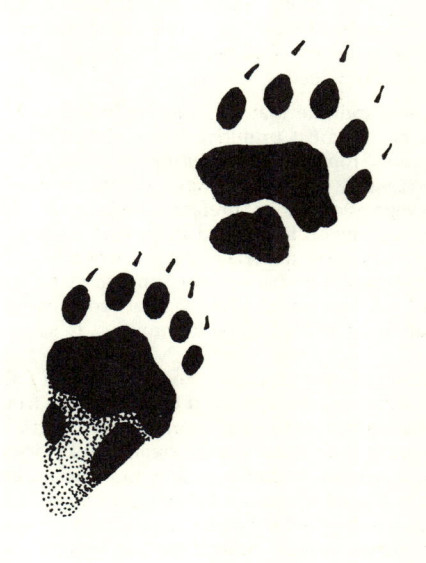

Western Spotted Skunk
life size in mud

MOUNTAIN BEAVER
Aplodontia
Aplodontia rufa

Order: Rodentia (gnawing mammals). **Family:** Aplodontiidae, a single-species family. **Range and habitat:** portions of Cascade and Sierra Nevada ranges as far south as Kings Canyon National Park; in dense, usually very moist forests and thickets. **Size and weight:** 13 inches; 3 pounds. **Diet:** ferns, skunk cabbage, nettles, devil's club and variety of other available herbaceous foliage. **Sounds:** generally silent; occasionally whistles, grunts.

Fossil records indicate that this squatty little brown nearly tailless animal may be the most primitive living rodent. Its common name probably derives from its habit of biting off plant stalks with which it constructs extensive tunnels, runways and burrows within the dense streamside vegetation of its preferred habitat. It also occasionally climbs trees to gnaw off limbs, and strips bark from tree trunks, in its search for construction materials. Active year-round though usually nocturnal, the mountain-beaver can sometimes be seen during late summer and autumn days, when it is at work making piles of cut vegetation up to 2 feet high along its runways, to serve as winter food stores.

The mountain beaver has five toes on each of its distinctively shaped feet, although the truncated thumbs of the front feet are least likely to leave imprints. You will usually find the tracks of this quiet and unassuming little beast along stream banks or on hiking trails nearby. The mountain beaver is a slow-moving animal that leaves a trail of closely spaced tracks not apt to be confused with those of any other animal within similar habitat, and it seldom ventures far from its complex burrow system. Several ground squirrels of northern California leave tracks of like shape, though smaller, but all of them avoid dense forests and thickets, preferring open meadows and pastureland, or rocky slopes and ridges.

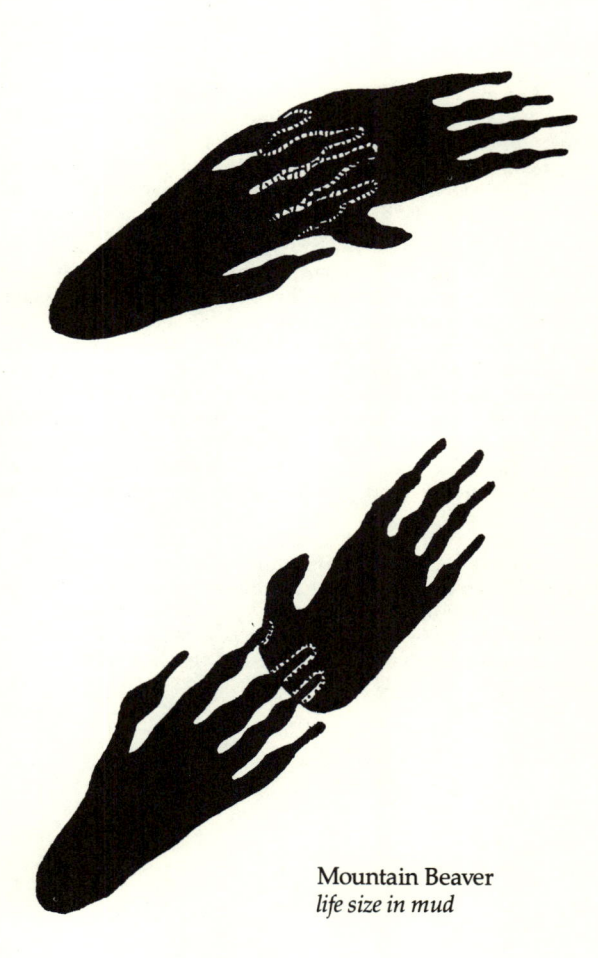

Mountain Beaver
life size in mud

MUSKRAT
Ondatra zibethicus

Order: Rodentia (gnawing mammals). **Family:** Cricetidae (New World rats and mice). **Range and habitat:** near Mount Shasta and Lassen Peak; in the northern and eastern portions of the state; in streams, lakes, ponds, and marshes. **Size and weight:** 24 inches; 4 pounds. **Diet:** aquatic vegetation; occasionally shellfish and small aquatic animals. **Sounds:** high-pitched squeaks.

The muskrat is a large brown rat with a volelike appearance, modified for its aquatic life by a rudderlike scaly tail and partially webbed hind feet. Muskrats associate readily with beavers and occasionally nest within the superstructure of beaver lodges. More often, muskrats burrow into riverbanks or construct lodges similar to those of beavers but extending only a couple of feet above water level and composed of aquatic vegetation, primarily grasses and reeds, rather than parts of trees. Muskrat lodges always have underwater entrances. Mainly nocturnal, the muskrat can be seen during the later afternoon or at dusk, pulling the V of its ripples across a still water surface, tail skulling behind, mouth full of grass for supper or nest-building.

Muskrat tracks are nearly always found in mud close to water. The muskrat is one of the few rodents with five toes on its front feet, but its truncated inner toes often leave no imprint. It leaves tracks about 2 inches apart when walking to 12 inches apart when running, with the tail sometimes dragging as well. The track of the hind foot is usually more distinctive than that of the front, and the stiff webbing of hair between the toes is often visible.

Muskrat
life size in mud

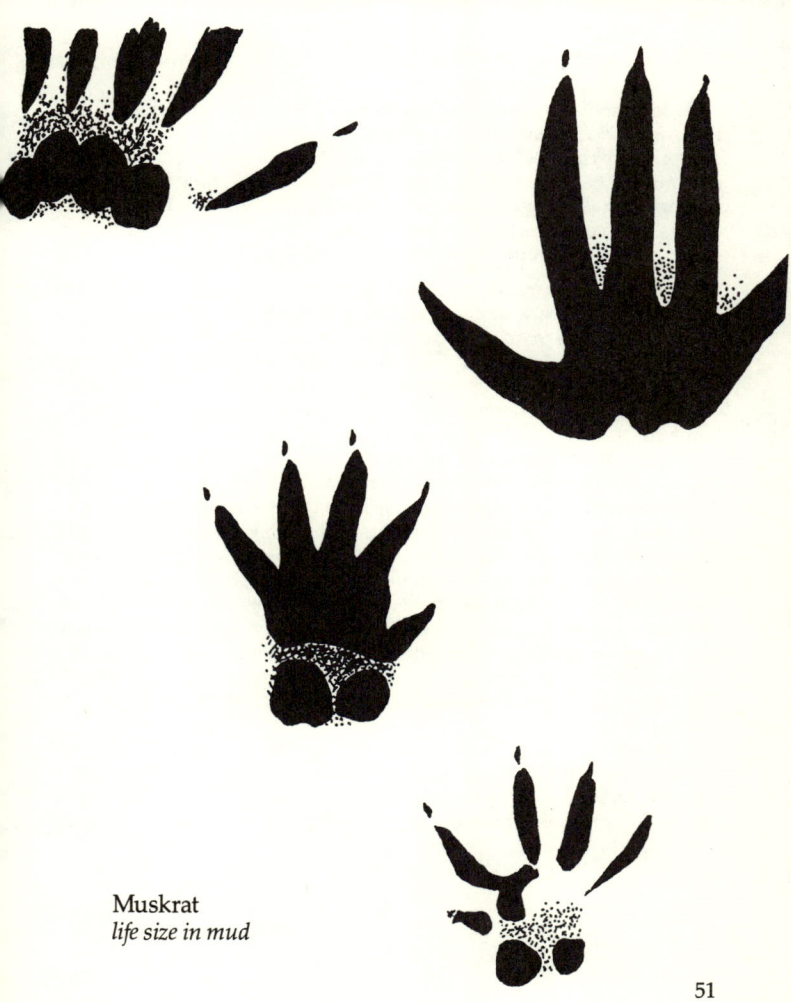

WESTERN GRAY SQUIRREL   *Sciurus griseus*

Order: Rodentia (gnawing mammals). **Family:** Sciuridae (squirrels). **Range and habitat:** widespread throughout most of California except the extremely arid regions; in hardwood (especially oak), pine, or mixed hardwood–evergreen forests, occasionally nearby in swamp fringes. **Size and weight:** 20 inches; 1.5 pounds. **Diet:** mostly acorns and cone seeds, also various nuts, fungi, insects and larvae, some vegetation. **Sounds:** variety of rapid, raspy barks.

This large, light-gray squirrel with its long upraised bushy tail is such a common park animal that most Californians are familiar with it. Active all day, year round, the western gray squirrel nests in tree cavities, or in conspicuous nests made of sticks and shredded bark, usually 20 feet or more above the ground. It spends a lot of time on the ground searching for nuts and seeds, and ranges widely from its home trees.

Because of its wandering habits, the western gray squirrel leaves a lot of tracks in areas traveled through by other similar-sized animals. Consequently, partial track impressions can be confusing. Most of the time, the gray squirrel scampers rather than walks, so its long rear heels don't leave prints. The real keys to recognizing the tracks of a western gray squirrel are the number of toes—four on the front feet, and five on the rear—and general track characteristics common to all members of the squirrel family. First, impressions of the entire toes, rather than just the tips, are often present. Second, two middle toes of the front feet and the three middle toes of rear feet are nearly always in line with, and parallel to, the heel pads, with the outer toes splayed out to the sides.

Track sets are normally about 4.5 inches wide and spaced 2 to 3 feet apart. After having determined the track in question belongs to a squirrel, rather than, say, one of the smaller weasels, then the size of the track should certainly indicate whether it was made by the gray squirrel.

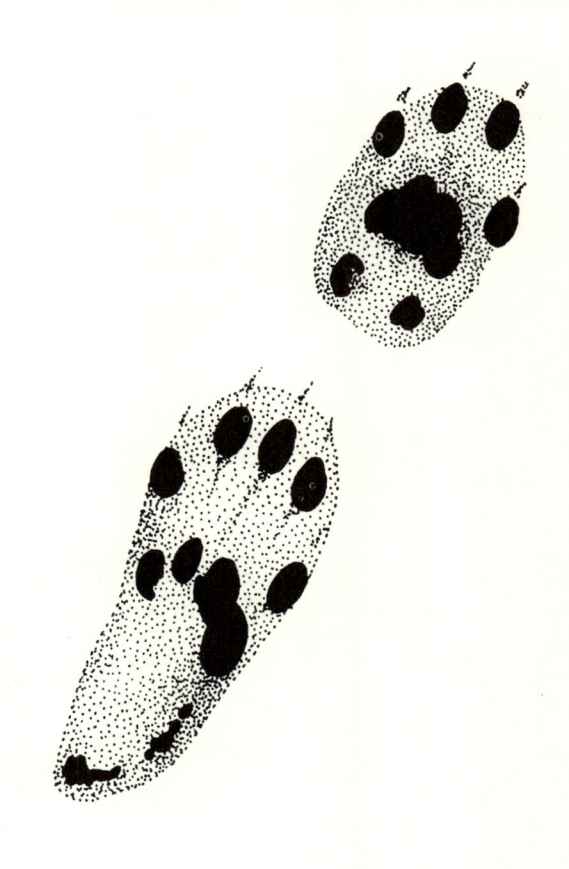

Western Gray Squirrel
life size in mud

VIRGINIA OPOSSUM   *Didelphis virginiana*

Order: Marsupialia (pouched mammals). **Family:** Didelphiidae. **Range and habitat:** most parts of the state west of the Sierra and deserts; in woodlands and adjoining areas, and farmlands, generally remaining near streams and lakes; also common around human habitations. **Size and weight:** 25 inches; 12 pounds. **Diet:** this opportunistic omnivore prefers fruits, vegetables, insects, small mammals, birds, eggs, carrion; also garbage and pet food. **Sounds:** a gurgling hiss when annoyed.

The generally nocturnal opossum appears fairly ordinary: it looks like a large, long-haired rat, with pointed nose, pale-gray fur, and a long, scaly, reptilian tail. Primarily terrestrial, the opossum may nest in an abandoned burrow or a fallen tree, but will climb to escape danger. Other than climbing, its only defense mechanism is an ability to feign death, or "play possum."

In many respects, however, the opossum is the most peculiar animal residing on this continent. Among the oldest and most primitive of all living mammals, it is the only animal in North America with a prehensile (grasping) tail, the only nonprimate in the animal kingdom with an opposable (thumblike) digit (the inside toes on the hind feet), and the only marsupial on the continent. As many as 14 young are born prematurely after only 13 days of gestation, weighing 1/15 ounce each (the whole litter would fit into a teaspoon!). The tiny babies crawl into their mother's pouch, where they remain for the next two months. After emerging from the pouch, they often ride around on the mother's back for some time. All of this is pretty unusual behavior, even in California.

Opossums leave easily identifiable tracks: the opposable hind thumb usually points 90 degrees or more away from the direction of travel, and the five front toes spread widely. Like raccoons, opossums leave tracks in a row of pairs. Each pair consists of one front- and one rear-foot imprint, always close to or slightly overlapping each other, and the pairs are from 5 to 11 inches apart, depending on size and speed. The opossum's long tail frequently leaves drag marks on soft surfaces.

Virginia Opossum
life size in mud

YELLOW-BELLIED MARMOT *Marmota flaviventris*
Mountain marmot, rockchuck, whistler

Order: Rodentia (gnawing mammals). **Family:** Sciuridae (squirrels). **Range and habitat:** Sierra Nevada northward through the Cascade Range; among talus slopes and rocky outcroppings in valleys, foothills, and mountainous regions, up to about 12,000 feet elevation. **Size and weight:** 18 inches; 10 pounds. **Diet:** prefers alfalfa; also succulent alpine grasses, plants, and flowers. **Sounds:** loud and high-pitched chirps at short intervals, and whistles.

The yellow-bellied marmot is a large, pretty American ground squirrel covered with light blond fur, with a distinctly yellowish neck and belly. Marmots lead lives of inertia, hibernating from August or September through February or March, sleeping at night during the short high-country summer, and spending the daytime eating or sunbathing on prominent lookout rocks. Fairly easy to find in the mountains, marmots betray their presence with piercing whistles, employed as both an alarm and to keep tabs on fellow marmots' locations. Their eyesight is not particularly good; by staying downwind and moving slowly, you should have no trouble sneaking up on them for a closer look.

When they walk, yellow-bellied marmots leave tracks that often intermingle and overlap. The illustration shows the four toes of the front foot and the five of the rear, a configuration typical of rodents. The rear foot is actually larger than the front one, but very often, especially when the marmot is running, the heel does not touch the ground. For this reason, the hind-foot track could be mistaken for the front footprint of a small raccoon. Typically, yellow-bellied marmot tracks are less than 2 inches long, with from 3 to 14 inches between clusters, depending on the speed of movement. Don't look for them on snow; marmots will be asleep through the snow season.

Yellow-bellied Marmot
life size in mud

RINGTAIL *Bassariscus astutus*
Ringtail Cat, Miner's Cat, Civet Cat, Cacomistle

Order: Carnivora (flesh-eating mammals). **Family:** Bassariscidae (ringtails). **Range and habitat:** throughout most of the state except central San Joaquin Valley area; most common in chaparral, rocky ridges, caves and cliffs, talus slopes, occasionally in forested areas. **Size and weight:** 30 inches, half of which is tail; 2 pounds. **Diet:** small animals, bats, birds, insects, fruit. **Sounds:** a coughing bark or whimper when alarmed.

The secretive, seldom seen ringtail has large round ears, white eye rings, an elongated gray body, and a distinctive bushy black-and-white-striped tail that is fully as long as its body. This strictly nocturnal animal tends to lead a solitary, inconspicuous life in relatively isolated terrain.

Ringtail tracks are uncommon and, when found, are not easy to distinguish from those of the spotted skunk. Because ringtails have semi-retractile claws, their tracks are often quite catlike, whereas those of spotted skunks usually show claw marks. Ringtail pad imprints also tend to be less elongated than those of the spotted skunks, ringtails are more likely to leave tail brush marks than spotted skunks, and ringtails usually leave doubled-over track pairs 6 to 10 inches apart, while spotted skunks leave very irregular trails of single prints, or clusters of four tracks.

Ringtail
life size in mud

MARTEN
Pine marten, American sable
Martes americana

Order: Carnivora (flesh-eating mammals). **Family:** Mustelidae (the weasel family). **Range and habitat:** Klamath Mountains, Cascades, Sierra Nevada; in coniferous forests, occasionally in adjoining areas, including rock slides. **Size and weight:** 30 inches; 3 pounds. **Diet:** primarily red squirrels; also other small mammals, birds, eggs, berries, and nuts. **Sounds:** generally silent.

Between a mink and a fisher in size, the energetic and adaptable marten is typically weasel-shaped, buff-colored on its throat and brownish or rusty-brown over the rest of its body, with a long, fluffy tail. Solitary, generally nocturnal, and always extremely wary, it is seldom sighted in the wild, but it is also inquisitive and can be lured from its den with squeaking, mouselike noises made by kissing the back of your hand. The marten covers distances of many miles in a single night's hunting and is active year round. A skillful tree climber, it spends a lot of time off the ground and often dens in tree cavities; the marten can nearly always be found in forests inhabited by the Douglas' squirrel.

The marten leaves few signs in the summer forest except for scat stations, spots where droppings are repeatedly left. On snow, its tracks are very similar to but slightly larger than mink tracks. Small, thin pads behind five toes and nails are normally visible in marten tracks, with size and spacing somewhat larger than that of the mink. Marten tracks, however, will tend to lead to and from trees and rarely venture near water, unlike the mink's. Walking tracks are usually 6 to 9 inches apart, running clusters 24 inches apart, and bounding pairs of overlapping prints as much as 40 inches apart.

Marten
life size in mud

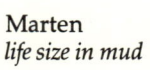

61

STRIPED SKUNK *Mephitis mephitis*

Order: Carnivora (flesh-eating mammals). **Family:** Mustelidae (weasels and skunks). **Range and habitat:** throughout California; in semi-open country, mixed woods, brushland, and open fields. **Size and weight:** 24 inches; 10 pounds. **Diet:** omnivorous, including mice, eggs, insects, grubs, fruit, carrion. **Sounds:** usually silent.

Often found dead along highways, this cat-sized skunk is easily recognized by the two broad stripes running the length of its back, meeting at head and shoulders to form a cap. A thin white stripe runs down its face. Active year round, it is chiefly nocturnal but may be sighted shortly after sunset or at dawn, snuffling around for food. It seeks shelter beneath buildings as well as in ground burrows or other protected den sites, and protects itself, when threatened, with a fine spray of extremely irritating methyl mercaptan; everyone knows what that smells like.

Striped skunk tracks are similar to but larger than those of the smaller spotted skunk, and its elongated heel pads are more often apparent because it's not as quick, agile, or highstrung as its smaller cousin. With five closely spaced toes and claws on all feet usually leaving marks, its tracks can't be mistaken for any others of its size; the spacing is distinctive too: generally less than six inches between track groups, whether they consist of walking pairs or strung-out loping groups of four tracks.

Striped Skunk
life size in mud

BULLFROG *Rana catesbiana*

Order: Salientia (frogs, toads, and allies). **Family:** Ranidae (true frogs). **Range and habitat:** widespread throughout most of California; in ponds, lakes, marshes and swamps, year-round bodies of water. **Size and weight:** body 5–8 inches, with long legs; 4 ounces. **Diet:** insects. **Sounds:** low-pitched croaks, deep jug-o-rum, especially at dawn and dusk.

Of the eighty-one species of frogs that live north of Mexico, the bullfrog is the largest. Varying in color from a mottled darker-gray to green, with an off-white belly, bullfrogs live in or very near water because they must keep their skin wet and they breed in water. They use distinctive vocalizations to signal each other and to attract mates. The 4-to-6-inch-long vegetarian tadpoles take up to two years to transform into carnivorous adults. As with all toads and frogs, be sure your hands are free from insect repellent or other caustic substances before you handle a bullfrog as it has particularly sensitive skin.

Frogs walk or hop in a more plantigrade manner than toads, so their tracks tend to be more easily recognizable. You will commonly find impressions of the full soles of their feet and might even be able to see that their hind feet are webbed, except the last joint of the longest toe, although these delicate membranes don't always imprint. The toed-in imprints of the small front feet combined with a straddle of 5 or 6 inches should leave no doubt about the identity of bullfrog tracks, even if the hind-foot impressions are less than distinct.

Only two other true frogs live in California, both primarily in the western half of the state. The tracks of the red-legged frog and yellow-legged frog are nearly identical to those of the bullfrog in shape, but considerably smaller in foot size, width of straddle, length of stride and leaps, and depth of impression in soft surfaces.

Bullfrog
2/3 life size in mud

BOBCAT
Wildcat

Felis rufus

Order: Carnivora (flesh-eating mammals). **Family:** Felidae (cats). **Range and habitat:** throughout California; in forested foothills, swamps and fringes, rimrock, and chaparral. **Size and weight:** 30 inches; 35 pounds. **Diet:** small mammals and birds; rarely carrion. **Sounds:** less vocal than the lynx, but capable of generic cat-family range of noises.

The bobcat is a very adaptable feline, afield both day and night and wandering as much as 50 miles in a day of hunting, occasionally into suburban areas. It is primarily a ground hunter, but will climb trees and drop onto unexpecting prey if the opportunity presents itself. You could mistake it for a large tabby cat with a bobbed tail, but the similarity ends there, for the bobcat has quite a wild disposition combined with greater size, strength and razor-sharp claws and teeth.

You can expect to encounter bobcat tracks almost anywhere. You'll know the roundish tracks belong to a cat because the retractile claws never leave imprints and the toes usually spread a bit more than a dog's. Bobcat tracks are too large to be mistaken for those of a domestic cat, however. The animal's weight will have set the tracks deeper in a soft surface than you would expect from a housecat, and domestic cats have pads that are single-lobed at the front end. Bobcat tracks are clearly smaller than those of a mountain lion and are therefore easily identifiable by process of elimination.

Bobcat
life size in mud

GRAY FOX *Urocyon cinereoargenteus*

Order: Carnivora (flesh-eating mammals). **Family:** Canidae (dogs). **Range and habitat:** throughout California in chaparral and brushy, sparsely wooded rimrock country. **Size and weight:** 40–42 inches; 12–15 pounds. **Diet:** omnivorous, including small mammals, birds, insects, eggs, fruit, nuts, grains, and other forage. **Sounds:** normally silent; occasionally short barking yips.

This pretty fox with gray back, rusty flanks, and white underside is generally nocturnal and secretive, but you might spot one foraging by daylight in thick foliage or forested areas. The only canine in America with the ability to climb, it frequently seeks refuge and food in trees, but cottontails are the mainstay of its diet when they are available. The gray fox typically dens among boulders on the slopes of rocky ridges or in rock piles, hollow logs, or the like; it uses these dens in winter as well as summer.

Gray fox tracks are usually distinct due to the relative lack of fur on the animal's feet. The tracks always show the imprints of claws with 7 to 12 inches between walking prints.

Gray Fox
life size in mud

COYOTE
Brush wolf, prairie wolf
Canis latrans

Order: Carnivora (flesh-eating mammals). **Family:** Canidae (dogs). **Range and habitat:** widespread throughout California; primarily in prairies, open woodlands, and brushy fringes, but very adaptable; can turn up anywhere. **Size and weight:** 48 inches; 45 pounds. **Diet:** omnivorous, including rodents and other small mammals, fish, carrion, insects, berries, grains, nuts, and vegetation. **Sounds:** wide range of canine sounds; most often heard yelping in group chorus late at night.

An important controller of small rodents, the smart, adaptable coyote is—unlike the gray wolf—steadily expanding its range. About the size of a collie, the coyote is a good runner and swimmer and has great stamina. Despite its wide range, it is shy, and you will be lucky to see one in the wild.

Typically canine, the coyote's front paw is slightly larger than the rear, and the front toes tend to spread wider, though not as wide as the bobcat's. The toenails nearly always leave imprints. The shape of coyote pads is unique, the front pads differing markedly from the rear, as shown, and the outer toes are usually slightly larger than the inner toes on each foot. The coyote tends to walk in a straight line and keep its tail down, which often leaves an imprint in deep snow. These characteristics plus walking strides of 8 to 16 inches and leaps to 10 feet may help you distinguish coyote tracks from those of domestic dogs with feet of the same size.

Coyote
life size in mud

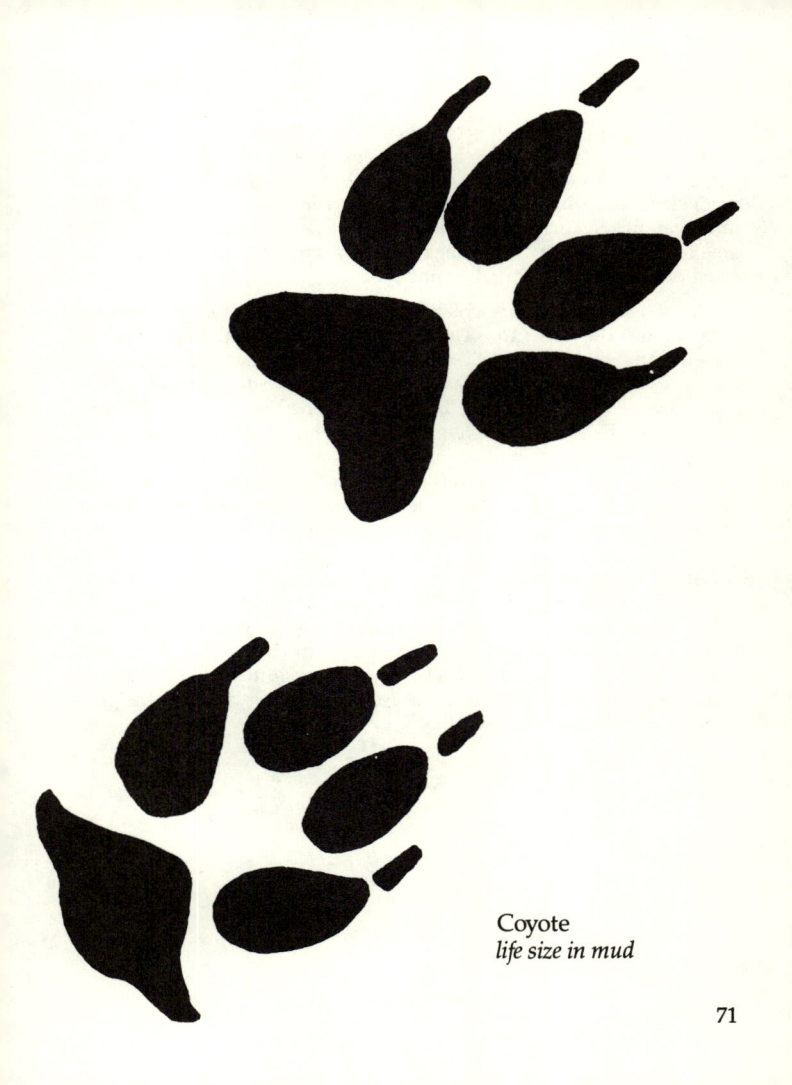

BADGER
Taxidea taxus

Order: Carnivora (flesh-eating mammals). **Family:** Mustelidae (the weasel family). **Range and habitat:** widespread throughout California; in treeless meadows, semiopen prairies, grasslands, and deserts at all altitudes, wherever ground-dwelling rodents are abundant. **Size and weight:** 28 inches; 20 pounds. **Diet:** carnivorous, including all small rodents, snakes, birds, eggs, insects, and carrion. **Sounds:** may snarl or hiss when alarmed or annoyed.

The badger is a solitary creature that digs up most of its food and tunnels into the earth to escape danger. Its powerful short legs and long strong claws are well suited to its earth-moving ways, and badgers can reputedly dig faster than a man with a shovel. Above ground the badger is a fierce fighter threatened only by much larger carnivores. The animal is active in daylight and not too shy, even entering campgrounds in its search for food. Its facial markings are quite distinctive and easily recognized: the face is black with white ears and cheeks and a white stripe running from its nose over the top of its head. The rest of the body is light brown or gray, and the feet are black.

Badger tracks show five long, clear toe prints of each foot and obvious marks left by the long front claws. The animal walks on its soles, which may or may not leave complete prints. Its pigeon-toed trail may be confused with the porcupine's in deep snow, but a porcupine trail will invariably lead to a tree or into a natural den, a badger's to a burrow of its own excavation; another clue: the badger's short, soft tail rarely leaves a mark.

Badger
life size in mud

FISHER
Black cat
Martes pennanti

Order: Carnivora (flesh-eating mammals). **Family:** Mustelidae (the weasel family). **Range and habitat:** portions of mountains of northern and eastern California south through Sierra Nevada; in coniferous and mixed forests and occasionally in cutover areas, usually at lower elevations. **Size and weight:** 36 inches; 15 pounds. **Diet:** primarily smaller mammals, including porcupines; also insects, birds, eggs, fish, frogs, and, infrequently, fruit and vegetation. **Sounds:** hisses, growls, and snarls.

The fisher likes fish when it finds them washed ashore, but will not enter water to catch them. This dark brown weasel with its foot-long bushy, tapering tail is slightly larger than the marten, more adaptable in habitat, and wider ranging, covering a territory of 150 square miles or more. Very aggressive and strong for its size, the fisher is terrifically speedy whether on the ground or climbing, all of which may explain why it is among the few predators that kill and eat porcupines regularly. Its diet also includes other weasel-family relatives.

Because the fisher is fairly scarce, nocturnal, and prefers wild mature forests, you will be very lucky to sight one in its natural habitat, but it is active year round and its tracks are easy enough to recognize. Typical of the weasel clan, all five toes and claws usually leave imprints, as do the rather narrow pads. Fisher tracks generally lead to or away from trees and avoid water. Walking stride is 5 to 7 inches, with clusters of running tracks 3 to 4 feet apart and 3 to 6 feet between leaping pairs of overlapping prints in the common weasel mode.

Fisher
life size in mud

PORCUPINE
Porky, quill pig
Erethizon dorsatum

Order: Rodentia (gnawing mammals). **Family:** Erethizontidae (porcupines). **Range and habitat:** widespread throughout northern and eastern California; usually in forested areas, also in brushy fringes, fields, meadows, and semidesert areas; a very adaptable animal. **Size and weight:** 30 inches; 25 pounds. **Diet:** vegetarian, including bark, leaves, fruits, berries, nuts, flowers. **Sounds:** normally quiet, capable of a great variety of grunts, whines, harmonicalike noises and rapid teeth clicking.

The porcupine is one of the few animals whose tracks you can follow with reasonable expectation of catching up with their maker. Often out during daylight hours, it moves quite slowly if not alarmed, stops frequently to nibble at vegetation, and does not see well, so if you're quiet, you can usually observe this peaceable animal at your and its leisure. An alarmed porcupine climbs a tree to escape danger, only using its quills as a last-ditch defense against an outright attack; and the porcupine cannot fling its quills, so there's no danger to any creature with enough sense to stay out of direct contact, a requisite that regrettably excludes many domestic dogs.

Often the porcupine's distinctive shuffling gait and dragging whisk-broom tail may be the only clear track signs it leaves behind, especially in deep snow. In winter, porcupine trails often lead to or away from a large coniferous tree, where the animal both sleeps and dines on bark and needles; alternatively, it may hole up in a den beneath a stump or in another ground-level shelter. Occasionally a piece of snow or mud that has stuck to a porcupine's foot will dislodge intact, revealing the unique pebbled texture of its soles. Imprints from the long claws are also often visible.

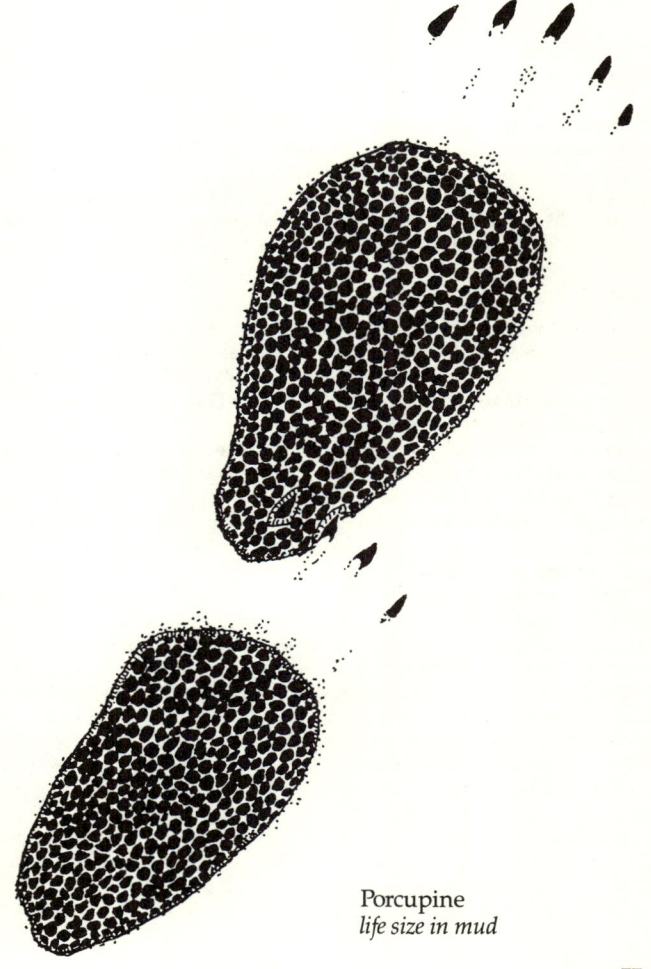

Porcupine
life size in mud

RACCOON
Coon
Procyon lotor

Order: Carnivora (flesh-eating mammals). **Family:** Procyonidae (raccoons, ringtails, and coatis). **Range and habitat:** throughout California except portions of the extremely arid southeast; in forest fringe and rocky areas near streams, ponds, and lakes. **Size and weight:** 36 inches; 25 pounds. **Diet:** omnivorous, including fish, amphibians, shellfish, insects, birds, eggs, mice, carrion, berries, nuts, and vegetation. **Sounds:** a variety of shrill cries, whistles, churrs, growls, and screeches.

From childhood most of us know the raccoon by its mask of black fur and its black tail stripes on an otherwise grayish-brown body. It's familiar as a character in kids' books and frontier lore, frequently seen as a road kill, and is both curious and bold enough to be a fairly common visitor to campgrounds and even residential homes nearly everywhere within its range. Chiefly nocturnal, raccoons are more commonly sighted in suburban neighborhoods raiding garbage cans and terrorizing family hounds than in wildlands. Interesting and intelligent animals with manual dexterity of great renown, raccoons are also reputed to make lively and intriguing pets, provided they are closely supervised.

Raccoons like to wash or tear food items apart in water, which apparently improves their manual sensitivity. Much of their food comes from aquatic prospecting, so you will often find their tracks near water. When a raccoon walks, its left rear foot is placed next to the right front foot, and so forth, forming paired track clusters. On firm mud or dirt, you will likely find tracks like those on the right, with distinct print details. On softer mud or wet spring snow, the tracks will look more like the two on the left. Running-track clusters tend to be bunched irregularly. The walking stride of a raccoon is about 7 inches; leaps average 20 inches.

The ringtail, which lives in rocky habitats around most of the state, could be mistaken for a raccoon at a quick glimpse. The ringtail's body is more foxlike, its face has white eye rings rather than a black mask, and its tail has black *and white* stripes. See pp. 58-59.

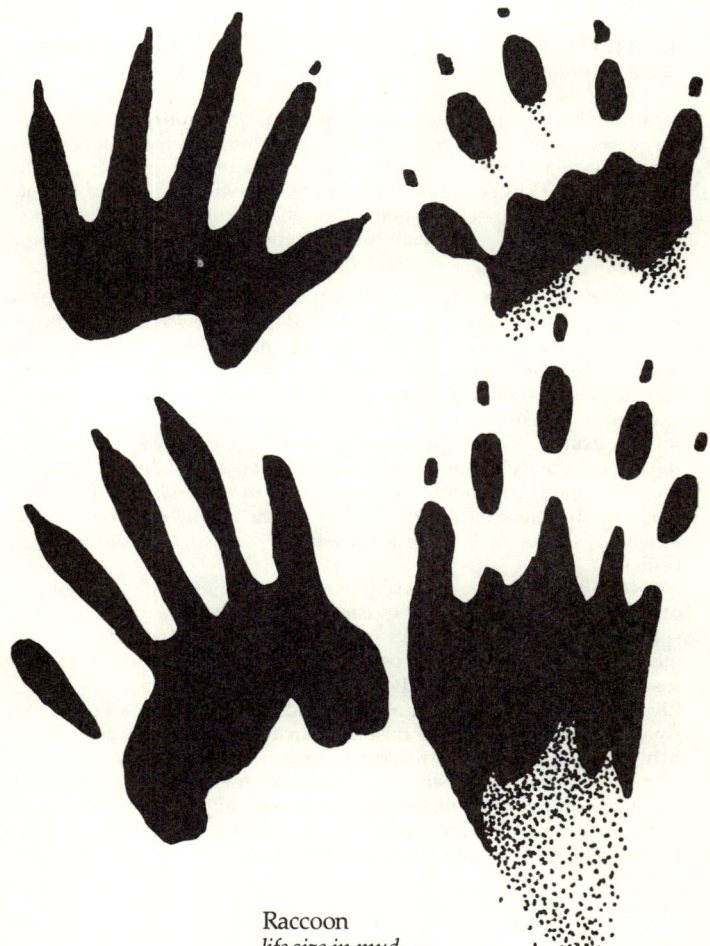

Raccoon
life size in mud

RIVER OTTER
Land otter
Lutra canadensis

Order: Carnivora (flesh-eating mammals). **Family:** Mustelidae (the weasel family). **Range and habitat:** uncommon throughout Northern California; portions of California north of Bakersfield; in and near lakes and streams. **Size and weight:** 48 inches; 25 pounds. **Diet:** fish, amphibians, shellfish and other aquatic invertebrates, snakes, turtles, birds, eggs. **Sounds:** chirps, chatters, chuckles, grunts, and growls.

The river otter is a dark brown weasel about as large as a medium-sized dog, with a thick, hairless tail adapted for swimming, much like that of the muskrat; in fact, the river otter closely resembles the muskrat in appearance and habitat, but is much larger, strictly carnivorous, and quite a bit more animated. Both in and out of water, alone or in the company of others, the river otter seems to be a graceful and exuberant, playful animal. Active during the daylight hours, the otter is wary of humans. Still, you might occasionally sight one in the wild; more commonly you may find, in summer, the flattened grass where otters have rolled, leaving their musky odor behind, or in winter, marks on snow or ice where they've playfully slid on their bellies.

River otter tracks are relatively easy to find and identify within the otter's range. The webs of the rear feet often leave distinct marks on soft surfaces, and claw marks usually are present. Individual tracks measure up to 3.5 inches across and due to their size cannot be confused with those of any other animal with similar aquatic habitat. River otters do venture into woodlands as well, however, where small otter tracks could be mistaken for those of a large fisher, but fisher tracks will lead to or from coniferous trees before long, in somewhat more linear patterns, while otter tracks meander, forming a trail roughly 8 to 10 inches wide and generally leading to or from water systems. Also, the river otter normally leaves groups of four tracks 13 to 30 inches apart, when it's not sliding on its belly.

River Otter
life size in mud

81

WOLVERINE
Glutton, skunk bear

Gulo gulo

Order: Carnivora (meat-eating mammals). **Family:** Mustelidae (weasels). **Range and habitat:** rare in Cascade and Sierra Nevada ranges south to Yosemite; in high-altitude forest, and boulder-strewn alpine meadows near and above timberline. **Size and weight:** 40 inches; 40 pounds. **Diet:** strictly carnivorous, including all smaller animals and carrion. **Sounds:** normally silent; may snarl or growl when disturbed.

This large weasel looks and acts like a small brown bear with a long, fluffy tail, buffy or gray cheeks and haunches, and the potential for a very nasty disposition. The wolverine is fierce, aggressive, and extremely strong for its size. Even black bears and mountain lions will avoid a confrontation with a healthy adult. Wary, secretive, inhabiting remote and desolate places, the wolverine is infrequently sighted in the wild.

A surprised wolverine may arch its back and dance sideways, much as a cat might, leaving all sorts of irregular track patterns in mud before disappearing beneath nearby boulders. Walking or scampering around, winter or summer, a wolverine leaves tracks that are easy to identify, being recognizably weasel-family and quite large; like other weasels, the wolverine walks flat-footed, and if not all of its soles leave marks, at least the heel knob behind the main pad usually does. The tracks also feature five toe marks with very distinct imprints of long, sharp claws. In high remote Californian habitat, no other tracks can be mistaken for those left by a wolverine.

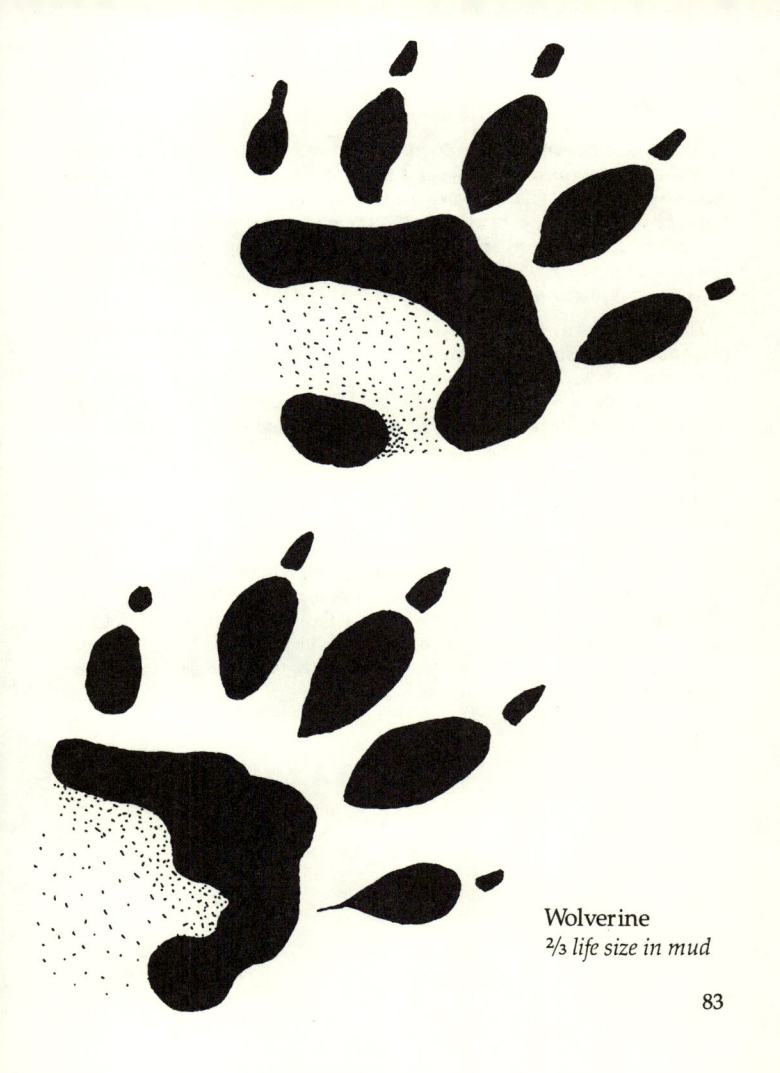

Wolverine
⅔ life size in mud

PRONGHORN
Antelope
Antilocapra americana

Order: Artiodactyla (even-toed hoofed mammals). **Family:** Antilocapridae (pronghorns). **Range and habitat:** Great Basin fringe areas of eastern California, particularly south and east of Death Valley; on open prairies and sagebrush plains. **Height and weight:** 36 inches at shoulder; 120 pounds. **Diet:** vegetation, including weeds, shrubs, grasses, and herbs; fond of sagebrush. **Sounds:** usually silent, but capable of a loud whistling sound when startled.

The pronghorn is the most easily observed of California's hoofed mammals. This sociable animal lives in flat open country, and its tan hide marked with striking white rump patches, a white underside, and facial spots is easy to recognize. The fastest animals in North America, pronghorns race around en masse at speeds of 45 miles per hour or so.

Because the pronghorn is easily sighted from a distance, you normally won't have to rely on tracks for identification, but the tracks should be easy to recognize because, unlike the mule deer which share much of its range, the pronghorn has no dewclaws. It is more gregarious than deer, and its running characteristics are unique: a large group of pronghorn may run for a mile or more in a straight line, whereas deer tend to run only when startled and then they don't run very far. The pronghorn's great speed produces an average separation of 14 feet between track clusters; running white-tailed deer average 6 feet, and mule deer average about 10 feet.

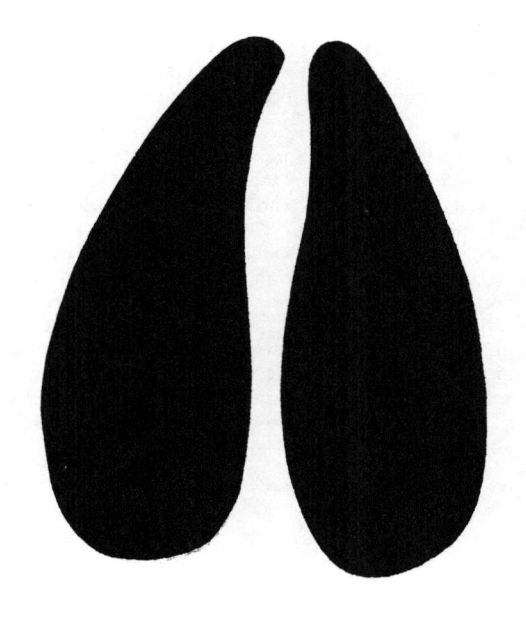

Pronghorn
life size in mud

MULE DEER *Odocoileus hemionus*

Order: Artiodactyla (even-toed hoofed mammals). **Family:** Cervidae (deer). **Range and habitat:** widespread throughout California; coniferous forests and adjoining areas at all elevations, regularly moving into grasslands, chaparral, and desert fringes that have browse plants available. **Height and weight:** 42 inches at shoulder; 350 pounds. **Diet:** herbivorous, including leaves, grasses, grains, nuts, and berries. **Sounds:** generally silent, but produces a snorting whistle when alarmed; makes occasional grunts and other vocal noises.

The mule deer is easily recognized by its large ears and black-tipped tail, which it holds down when running. Active during the day and at dusk, the mule deer can be observed fairly often in the wild. Skittish, at the first sign of alarm it flees with a unique feet-together bounding gait, all four hooves landing and taking off at the same time. This gait is an adaptation to life in rugged, often densely brushy terrain. The mule deer is also a strong swimmer.

Mule deer tracks show small, slender hooves usually spread slightly at the heels and, often, dewclaw impressions. The doubled-over walking tracks are usually less than 2 feet apart; at speeds beyond a walk, the mule deer does not trot like the white-tailed deer, but bounds, leaving very distinctive clusters of parallel tracks 10 feet or more apart.

Mule Deer
life size in mud

WILD BOAR *Sus scrofa*

Order: Artiodactyla (even-toed hoofed mammals). **Family:** Suidae (Old World swine). **Range and habitat:** San Luis Obispo County north to Marin and Sonoma counties; habitat variable, including dense forests, adjoining brushlands, dry hills, and swampy fringes, particularly in winter. **Height and weight:** 36 inches at shoulder; 300 pounds. **Diet:** acorns and other nuts, roots, grasses, fruit, also small amphibians, eggs, occasionally small mammals and carrion. **Sounds:** grunts and squeals typical of domestic pigs.

Wild boars were brought from Europe in 1925 to stock hunting preserves in Monterey County, where some inevitably escaped and bred with feral domestic pigs; today California's wild boars are almost entirely hybrids. These brown or gray creatures are recognizably piglike in shape, but their humped backs, shaggy coats, and formidable tusks readily distinguish them from domestic animals. Strong, agile, and occasionally aggressive, wild boars can be dangerous to encounter in the dense vegetation they tend to prefer. They are most active at dawn and dusk, are good swimmers and fast runners, and usually move about in family groups of 6 or so animals, occasionally congregating in herds of up to 50.

The cloven tracks of wild boars could be mistaken for those of mule deer, which overlap their range, but notice that wild boar tracks are more rounded, with toes more splayed, heels together—often to the extent that no break is apparent in the imprint at all, and dewclaw imprints, in soft ground, are farther out to the sides than you'd find in deer tracks. Wild boars have strides of about 18 inches, usually in a narrow line; they root around on the ground in their search for nuts and other food, leaving behind characteristic diggings, and rub or gouge trees with their tusks within 3 feet of the ground. Mule deer, on the other hand, leave narrower hoofprints with heels usually separated, 24-inch strides, and evidence of browsing foliage 5 or 6 feet above the ground.

Wild Boar
life size in mud

BIGHORN SHEEP *Ovis canadensis*
Desert bighorn, mountain sheep

Order: Artiodactyla (even-toed hoofed mammals). **Family:** Bovidae (cattle, sheep, and goats). **Range and habitat:** Great Basin fringe areas of eastern California, especially common in Death Valley National Monument and desert mountain ranges; in mountainous, sparsely populated terrain and high hilly desert, avoiding forested areas. **Height and weight:** 45 inches at shoulder; 275 pounds. **Diet:** variety of high-altitude browse, grasses, herbs, lichens. **Sounds:** most recognizable and voluminous are the sounds of head and horn butting made by competing rams during late fall; coughs, grunts, bleating.

This big sheep, with its distinctive white rump and heavy coiled horns, lives in remote areas of eastern California, where its hooves with their hard outer edge and spongy center give it excellent agility on rocky surfaces. It tends, however, to prefer high mountain meadows and scree slopes. In the summer, you commonly see groups of about ten ewes and lambs grazing or lying around chewing their cuds. In winter, rams join the herd, which may grow in size to 100 animals or more. The most distinctive behavior of the bighorn sheep is the frenzied, high-speed head butting engaged in by competing rams before the autumn mating season; noise from the impact carries a great distance in the open mountain country. Thanks to a certain American truck manufacturer's television ads, people have had the opportunity to witness this head-butting ram ritual without having to venture into remote mountainous wildlands, thus saving wear and tear on fragile ecosystems and human knee joints.

Because of the habitat where they are commonly found, bighorn sheep tracks are rarely confused with those of other hoofed animals. The hooves average 3.5 inches in length, longer than those of other deer but not as big as those of the elk. Rather blunt and square, the hooves may show signs of wear and tear from the scree slopes; dewclaw prints are never left.

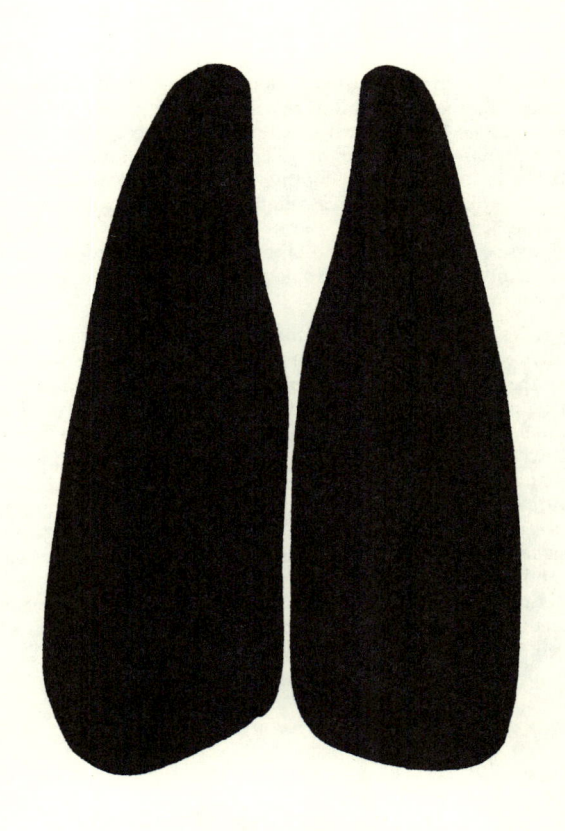

Bighorn Sheep
life size in mud

ELK
Wapiti
Cervus elaphus

Order: Artiodactyla (even-toed hoofed mammals). **Family:** Cervidae (deer). **Range and habitat:** portions of northwestern California west of Interstate 5 and south to Clear Lake, also rare in Inyo and Sequoia national forests, and the Sierra Madre Mountains north of Santa Barbara; in mountains, foothills, plains, valley meadows, and fringes of semiopen forests; at higher altitudes in summer than winter. **Height and weight:** 60 inches at shoulder; 900 pounds. **Diet:** leaves, grasses, bark, grains, and other vegetation. **Sounds:** variety of squeals, grunts, and barking exhalations; distinctive bugle call during autumn mating.

California's largest hoofed animal, the elk's numbers have been drastically reduced by hunters over the last century. The cow elk does not have the impressive multispiked antlers of the adult male, but all elk can be recognized easily: significantly larger than the mule deer, the elk has a mane noticeably darker than its body, yellowish-white rump patches, and a small white tail. Unlike the mule deer, the elk is a herd animal.

Individual elk tracks measure as much as 4.5 inches in length; the dewclaws may not leave imprints when the elk is walking, but on softer surfaces or when running, the elk's sheer weight drives its legs down, and the dewclaw prints will be apparent. The elk's walking gait measures from 25 to 30 inches; clusters of running tracks may be 4 to 8 feet apart. Shallow ponds and mud wallows are the best places to find elk tracks during the months when snow is absent.

Elk
life size in mud

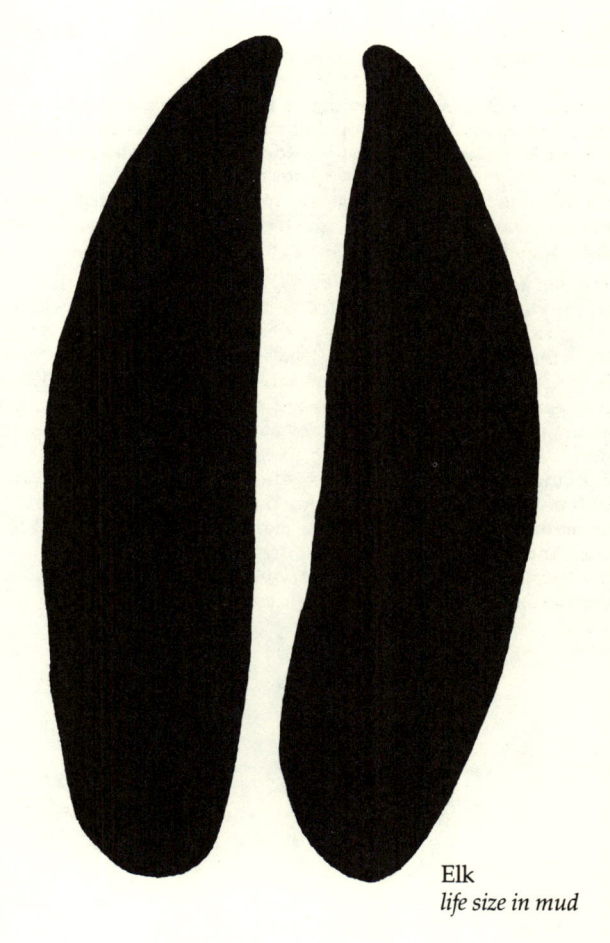

MOUNTAIN LION
Puma, cougar, panther, catamount
Felis concolor

Order: Carnivora (flesh-eating mammals). **Family:** Felidae (cats). **Range and habitat:** rare throughout most of California, absent from the central valleys; in rugged wilderness mountains, forests, and swamp fringes. **Size and weight:** 84 inches; 200 pounds. **Diet:** primarily deer, small mammals, and birds; occasionally domestic animals. **Sounds:** generally quiet, but capable of a variety of voluminous feline screams, hisses, and growls.

Hunted to the verge of extinction, our large, tawny, native American cat with its long, waving tail is now so scarce and secretive and is confined to such remote terrain that you'd be very lucky to sight one in the wild. But you at least have a chance to find the tracks of this big cat, which hunts mostly on the ground. It occasionally climbs trees, particularly to evade dogs but also to drop onto unwary prey (the mountain lion is an important natural control of the deer population).

Spacing of tracks will be what you'd expect of the large cat: trail width of 12 inches or more, walking tracks over 20 inches apart, 3 feet separating pairs of loping tracks, and bounding leaps of 12 feet or more. Another sure sign is the tail drag marks that may be found, especially in snow. Of course, like most cats, the mountain lion has retractile claws, which never leave marks.

Mountain Lion
life size in mud

MOUNTAIN COTTONTAIL
Nuttall's cottontail
Sylvilagus nuttalli

Order: Lagomorpha (rabbitlike mammals). **Family:** Leporidae (hares and rabbits). **Range and habitat:** most upland portions of eastern California; in mountainous sagebrush, thickets, rocky areas, and forests, often extending into outskirts of urban areas. **Size and weight:** 13 inches; 3 pounds. **Diet:** green vegetation, bark, twigs, sagebrush, and juniper berries. **Sounds:** usually silent; loud squeal when extremely distressed.

Cottontails are the pudgy, adorable rabbits with cottonball tails, known to us all from childhood tales of Peter Rabbit. Active day and night, year round, they're generally plentiful due in part to the fact that each adult female produces three or four litters of four to seven young rabbits every year. Of course, a variety of predators helps control their numbers, and few live more than a year in the wild.

Cottontail tracks are easily recognized because the basic pattern doesn't vary much, regardless of the rabbit's speed. It's important to note that, as with all rabbit-family tracks, sometimes the front feet land together, side by side, but just as often the second fore foot lands in line ahead of the first. The mountain cottontail leaves track clusters that span 6 and 9 inches normally, with up to 3 feet between running clusters.

You will have no problem telling cottontail tracks from those of jackrabbits, whose track clusters span as much as 2 feet, with up to 20 feet separating clusters; and because jackrabbits tend to run up on the toes of their hind feet, they often leave *smaller* hind foot imprints than cottontails do. The comparably great size of the snowshoe hare's feet makes its tracks easy to distinguish.

Similar tracks in open lowland valleys probably belong to the desert cottontail. In the chaparral of California's foothills, the brush rabbit is the resident cottontail. Finally, the pygmy rabbit frequents a small area of sagebrush along the eastern border of the state.

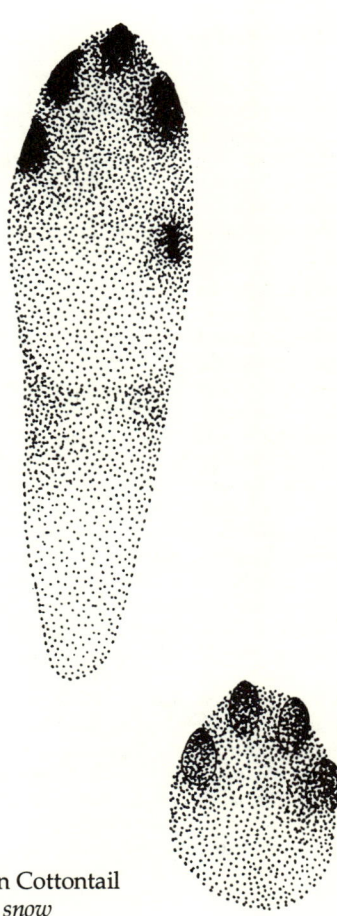

Mountain Cottontail
life size in snow

BLACK-TAILED JACKRABBIT *Lepus californicus*
Jackass rabbit

Order: Lagomorpha (rabbitlike mammals). **Family:** Leporidae (hares and rabbits). **Range and habitat:** throughout most of the state; in open prairies and sparsely vegetated sage and cactus country. **Size and weight:** 20 inches; 6 pounds. **Diet:** mostly grasses and other green vegetation, often along highway edges; also shrubs, buds, bark, twigs, and cultivated crops. **Sounds:** normally silent.

The black-tailed jackrabbit, the most widespread and numerous jackrabbit of California, is easily recognized by its year-round light gray fur, white underside, and distinctive black fur patch on top of its tail. It is most active from dusk to dawn and spends most of its days lying in depressions it scoops out at the base of a bush, by a rock, or at any other spot that gives it a bit of protection. These jackrabbits are sociable and are often seen feeding in small groups.

The white-tailed jackrabbit is found on the plains and foothills of northeastern California, ranging upslope to above the timberline in the Sierra Nevada. The tracks of both are indistinguishable where their ranges overlap. Front prints, about 3 inches long, are usually compact but often splayed, as shown; are usually the same size regardless of speed, and fall behind the rear, a pattern typical of all rabbits. Hind prints vary greatly in size. Walking slowly and flat-footed, jackrabbits leave narrow rear prints about 6 inches long, but as speed increases, heels lift until, at top speed of 35 to 40 miles per hour, only the toes leave prints, about 3.5 inches long, sometimes resembling coyote tracks.

Jackrabbit tracks cannot be confused with those of the snowshoe hare, which overlaps the ranges of both jackrabbits, because snowshoe hares prefer forested rather than open terrain and their toes are bigger and usually spread apart leaving larger imprints.

The most distinguishing track characteristic of jackrabbits is that, at speed, they leap from 7 to 12 feet or more. Coyotes and snowshoe hares rarely leap more than 6 feet, and cottontails bound no more than 3 feet.

Black-tailed Jackrabbit
½ life size in sand

SNOWSHOE HARE *Lepus americanus*
Varying hare

Order: Lagomorpha (rabbitlike mammals). **Family:** Leporidae (hares and rabbits). **Range and habitat:** the Cascade Range and south to Yosemite; in mountainous forests, brush thickets, and swamp fringes. **Size and weight:** 18 inches; 4 pounds. **Diet:** succulent vegetation in summer, twigs, bark, and buds in winter; occasionally east frozen meat. **Sounds:** generally silent; may thump feet, scream, grunt, or growl occasionally.

This medium-sized member of the rabbit family is active day and night year round and is quite common over a large territory within its preferred habitat. The animal has two color phases: medium brown in summer months, molting in winter to white—sometimes slightly mottled with brown—with black ear tips. Aptly named, its unique heavily furred hind feet have separable toes, allowing them to function like snowshoes when the hare is traveling on soft surfaces, especially deep snow.

Although its range partially overlaps that of both cottontails and jackrabbits, track recognition is easy because of the natural snowshoe formed by its toes. A snowshoe hare's toes always spread out, leaving distinctively separate imprints. Track measurements lie between the cottontail's and jackrabbit's: the length of each track cluster of four prints averages 11 inches; hopping distance is about 14 inches, and leaps are more than 5 feet.

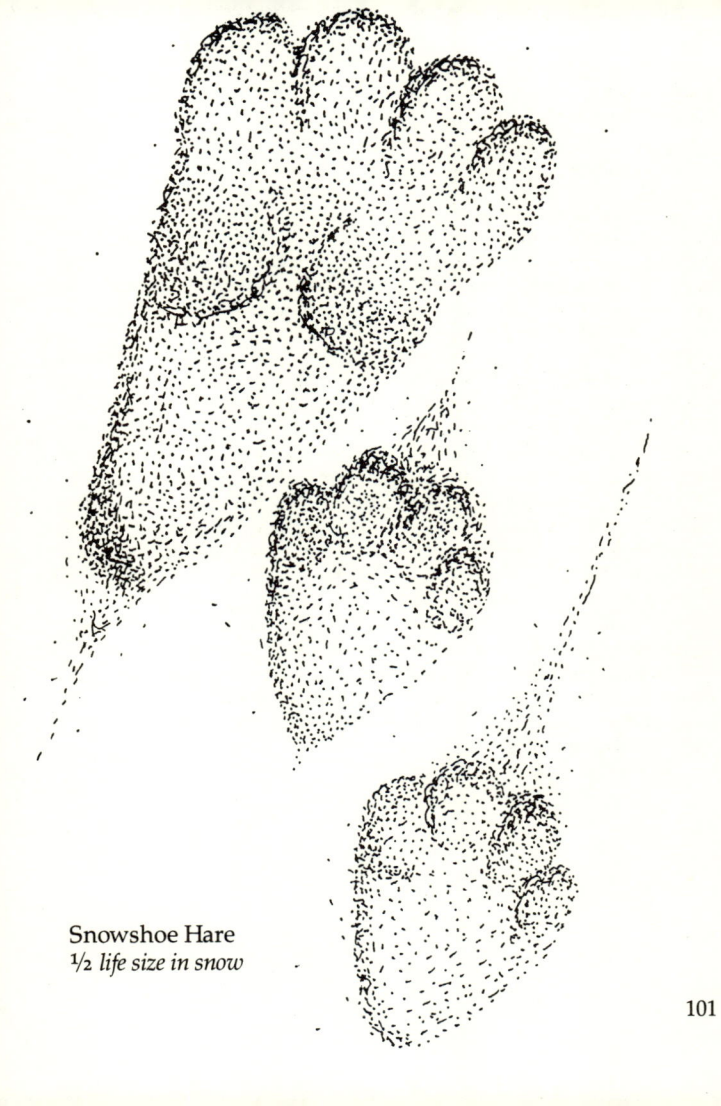

Snowshoe Hare
½ life size in snow

TURTLES
Order: Testudines

Forty-eight species of turtles live in North America. Their tracks are fairly common near bodies of water and, less frequently, in moist woodlands. These peculiar creatures predate dinosaurs and have a body structure unlike any other animal: a shell composed of expanded ribs, limbs extending from within the turtle's rib cage, and a horny beak instead of teeth. The shell is divided into two parts: the upper is called the carapace, and the lower, which is hinged in some species, is called the plastron.

The track left by a turtle is determined by the shape of the plastron and how high the turtle is holding its shell from the ground surface, which in turn depends on the species of turtle, the length of its legs, and the firmness of the surface it's walking over.

The track drawn on the left (the turtle moved toward the top of the page) shows that the turtle dragged most of its plastron, leaving a trail that obscured a lot of the indistinct prints left by its appendages; the drag trail looks similar to that of a tail-dragging beaver, but the shell-dragging turtle trail goes straight for several feet or more, until the turtle changes direction, whereas the beaver's tail-dragging trail zigzags slightly over 6 or 8 inches.

The second turtle trail, drawn on the right, was left on a firmer surface by a turtle who held its plastron off the surface; only the turtle's tail dragged, leaving a narrow, almost straight line. Individual footprints were merely smudges in some places, where the reptile had slipped, but where the turtle took firm steps, the tracks showed its feet and strong claws.

Turtles
1/10 life size in mud

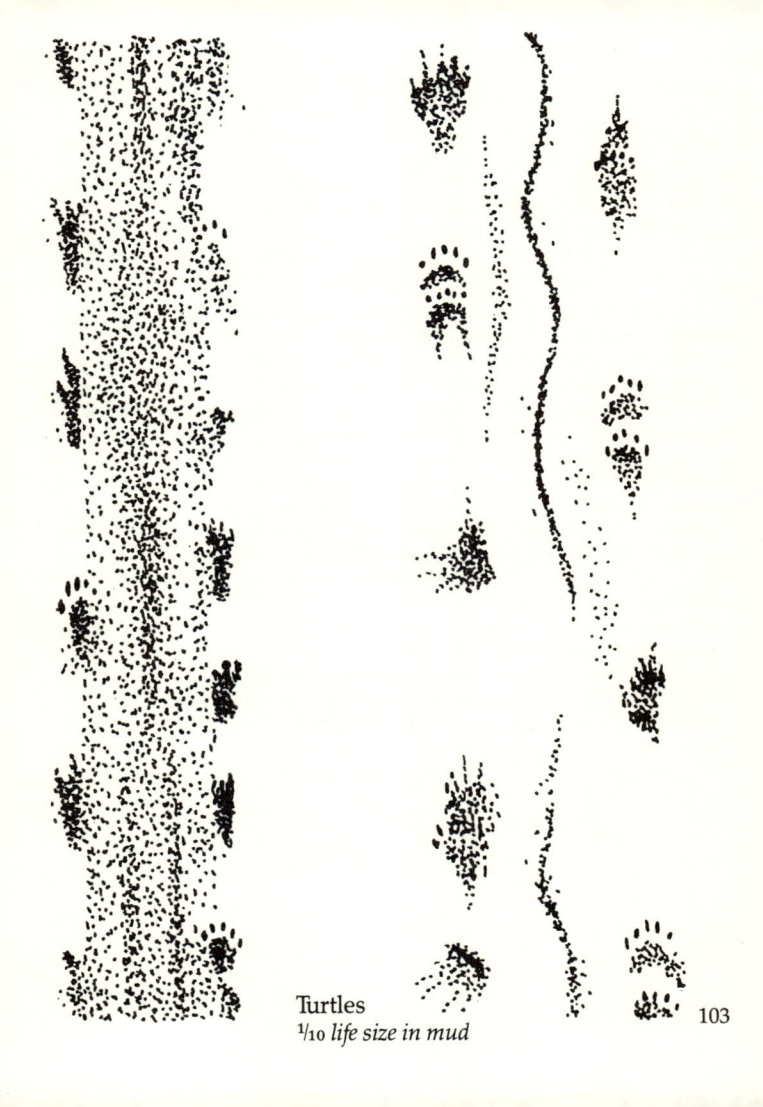

BEAVER
Castor canadensis

Order: Rodentia (gnawing mammals). **Family:** Castoridae (beavers). **Range and habitat:** northern California, mainly in Central Valley and Sierra; in streams and lakes with brush and trees or in open forest along riverbanks. **Size and weight:** 36 inches; 55 pounds. **Diet:** aquatic plants, bark, and the twigs and leaves of many shrubs and trees, preferably alder, cottonwood, and willow. **Sounds:** nonvocal, but smacks tail on water surface quite loudly to signal danger.

This industrious, aquatic mammal is the largest North American rodent. Although it sometimes lives unobtrusively in a riverbank, usually it constructs the familiar beaver lodge, a roughly conical pile of brush, stones, and mud extending as much as 6 feet above the surface of a pond, and gnaws down dozens of small softwood trees with which it constructs a conspicuous system of dams, often several hundred yards long. A beaver can grasp objects with its front paws and stand and walk upright on its hind feet. It uses its flat, scaly, strong tail for support out of water and as a rudder when swimming. Gregarious animals, beavers work well together on their collective projects. They are active day and night year round, but may operate unobserved beneath the ice during much of the winter, using subsurface lodge entrances.

If you are lucky, the large, webbed hind foot tracks left by a beaver will be clear, with 6 to 8 inches between pairs. Beavers frequently, however, obscure part or most of their tracks by dragging their tails and/or branches over them, leaving a trail much like that of a 6-inch-wide turtle, except the beaver's tail-drag trail zigzags slightly every 6 or 8 inches. The zigzag is the key to identification, as a turtle moves in reasonably long, straight segments until it changes direction significantly.

Beaver
½ life size in mud

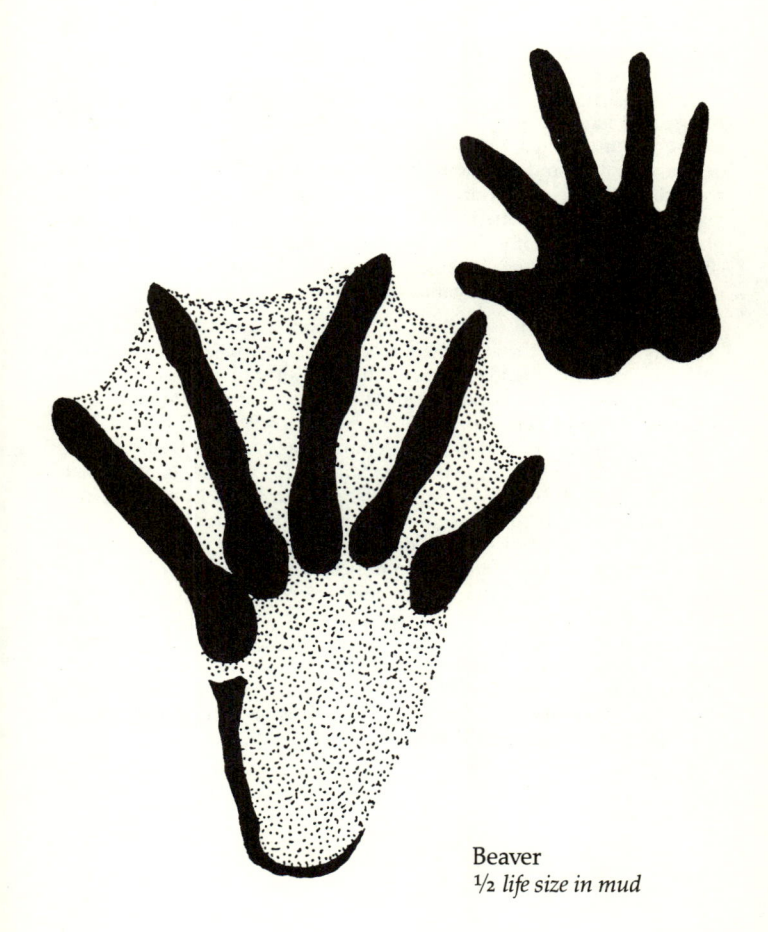

BLACK BEAR
Cinnamon bear

Ursus americanus

Order: Carnivora (flesh-eating mammals). **Family:** Ursidae (bears). **Range and habitat:** portions of northern and eastern California south to the mountains of Southern California; primarily in medium-to-higher elevation mountainous forests and swamp fringes. **Size and weight:** 6.5 feet; 450 pounds. **Diet:** omnivorous, including smaller mammals, fish, carrion, insects, fruit, berries, nuts, and succulent plants. **Sounds:** usually silent, but may growl, grunt, woof, whimper, click teeth, smack jaws together, or make other immediately recognizable indications of annoyance or alarm.

The black bear is the smallest and most common American bear. You may have seen these animals around rural garbage dumps and in parks. In the wild, the black bear is shy and wary of human contact as a general rule and thus not frequently sighted. If you do sight one, however, it can be very dangerous to underestimate it. The black bear is very strong, agile, and quick. It climbs trees, swims well, can run 25 miles per hour for short stretches, and above all else, is unpredictable. The black bear may seem docile and harmless in parks, but it has been known to chase people with great determination.

Be alert for bear trails, worn deep by generations of bear, and for trees with claw marks and other indications of bear territory. Bear tracks are usually easy to identify; they are roughly human in shape and size but slightly wider. The large claws leave prints wherever the toes do. If a bear slips on mud or ice, its soles leave distinctive smooth slide marks; nearby you will no doubt find more orderly tracks. Both adult black and immature grizzly bear tracks measure about 7 inches, but the grizzly bear, which is shown on California's state flag, was exterminated in the state in the 1920s.

Black Bear
½ life size in mud

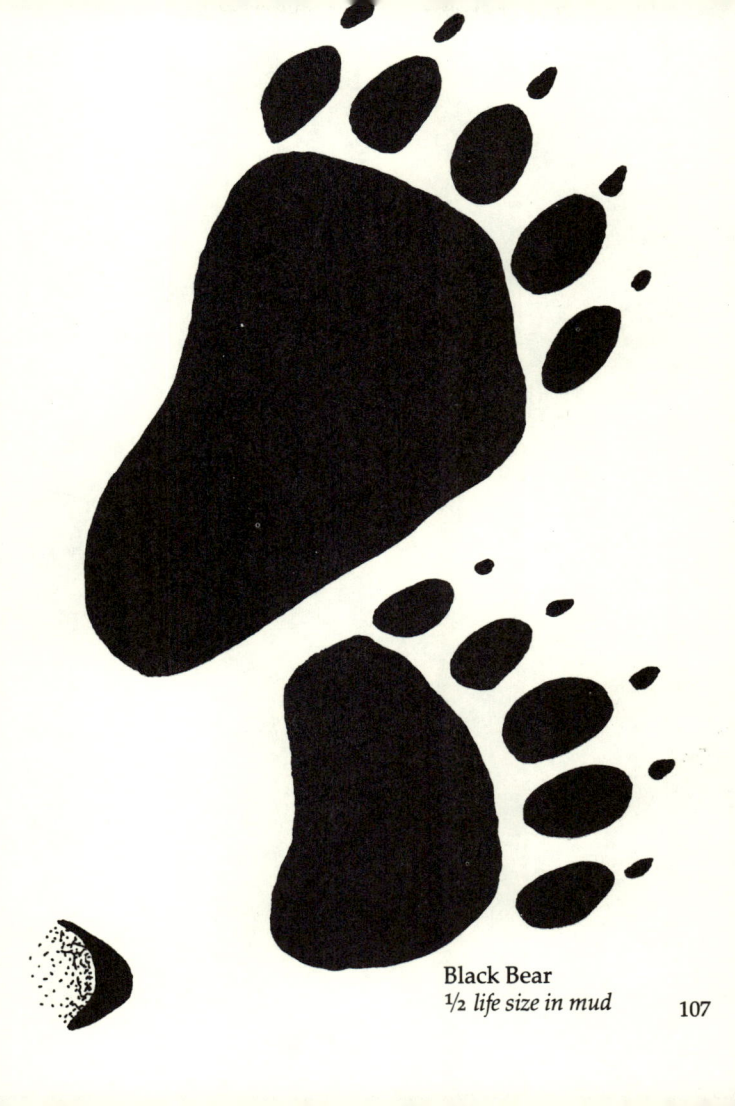

BIRDS

NORTHERN JUNCO

Junco hyemalis

Order: Passeriformes (perching birds). **Family:** Fringillidae (buntings, finches, and sparrows). **Range and habitat:** year-round in most of California; common in and near coniferous forests, weedy fields, brushy forest fringes. **Size and weight:** length 6 inches, wingspan 8 inches; less than 1 ounce. **Diet:** seeds, insects, and berries. **Sounds:** chips and trills.

The junco is the most common songbird in the conifer forest of California. In winter, small flocks of gray, brown, and white juncos migrate downslope out of the mountains to frequent backyards in the lowlands. Juncos are attracted to feeders but prefer to feed on the ground beneath them, relying on the ample seed spilled by the birds above.

Junco tracks are typical of the vast number of smaller land birds that leave delicate lines on snow, sand, or mud of inland areas. Hind toes are about twice as long as front toes, and the tracks are found in pairs spaced up to 5 inches apart, as these birds hop instead of walk. The relative size of the tracks will give a clue to the identity of the maker, as will the habitat and seasonal considerations, verified, of course, by actual field sightings.

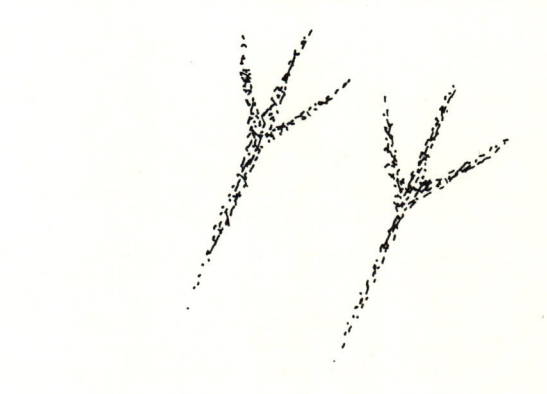

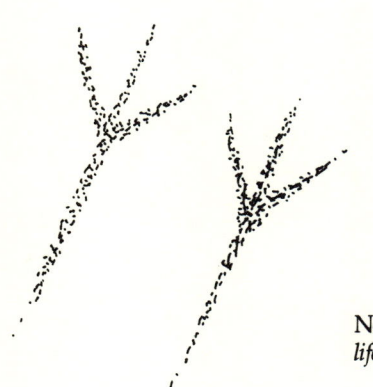

Northern Junco
life size in snow

KILLDEER
Charadrius vociferus

Order: Charadriiformes (shorebirds, gulls, and terns). **Family:** Charadriidae (plovers). **Range and habitat:** year-round in most of lowland California; common along shorelines, also found on inland fields and pastures. **Size and weight:** length 8 inches, wingspan 12 inches; 4 ounces. **Diet:** insects and larvae, earthworms, seeds. **Sounds:** repeats its names as its call.

The killdeer is one of the most common and recognizable shorebirds. Its two black breast bands are distinctive, as is its habit of feigning injury to lead intruders away from its nesting area. The killdeer is the only shorebird found year round in most of the region. Its tracks are typical as well of the tracks—usually found on damp sand—of shorebirds that visit the region seasonally: the front center toes is longer than the two outer toes; the small hind toe, more of a heel spur than a toe, leaves a small imprint; and the tracks are usually printed in a line, only an inch or two apart for birds the size of the killdeer, less for sandpipers, and up to 6 inches apart for birds the size of a greater yellowlegs. The general shape and lack of any evidence of webbing between the toes separate shorebird tracks from those of gulls or ducks.

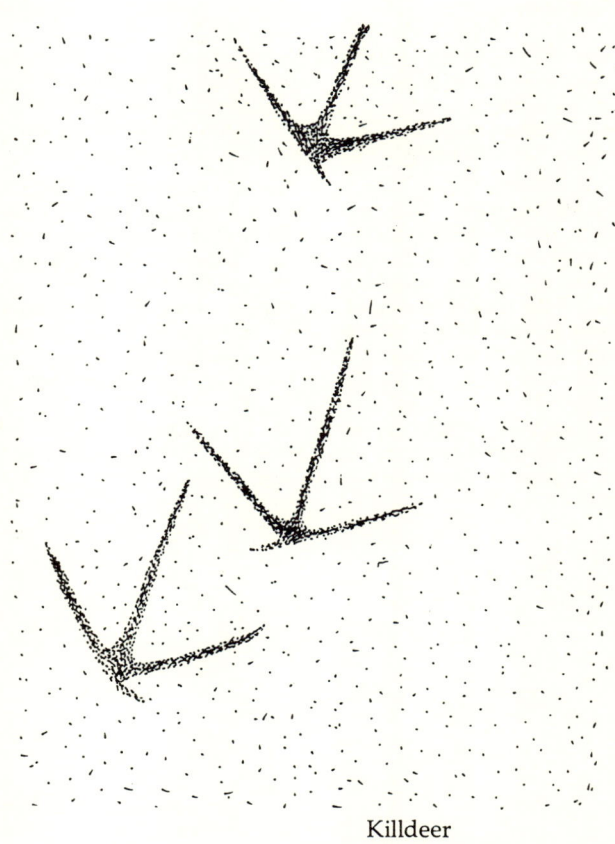

Killdeer
life size in sand

AMERICAN CROW   *Corvus brachyrhynchos*

Order: Passeriformes (perching birds). **Family:** Corvidae (jays, magpies, crows). **Range and habitat:** year-round throughout California; in all habitats except extremely arid regions. **Size and weight:** length 17 inches, wingspan 26 inches; 1 pound. **Diet:** nearly everything from mice to carrion to garbage. **Sounds:** distinctive "caw."

Crows are relatively intelligent birds, quite vocal, make good pets and can be taught to mimic human voices. Researchers have also determined that crows can count, and both wild and pet crows have been observed making up games to play. Watching crows will often help you locate other wildlife, too: groups of crows will mob and scold a predator such as an owl, for example, or perch near an offensive animal, darting in to harass and scold it. The common crow can be told from a distant hawk by its frequent steady flapping; it seldom glides more than 2 or 3 seconds except in strong updrafts or when descending.

All four of the crow's toes are about the same length, each with a strong claw, all of which leave prints most of the time. Crows walk and skip; their tracks are not usually made in pairs.

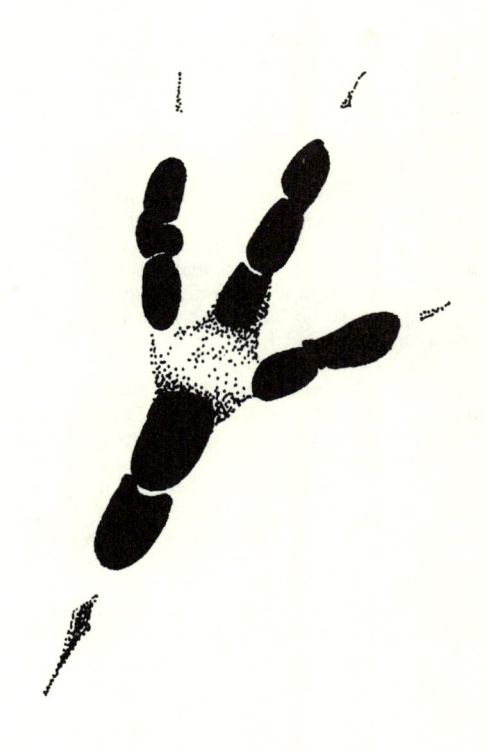

American Crow
life size in mud

MALLARD *Anas platyrhynchos*

Order: Anseriformes. **Family:** Anatidae (ducks, geese and swans).
Range and habitat: year-round resident of most of the northern half of the state; lakes, ponds, fresh-water marshes, and coastal waters.
Size and weight: length 28 inches, wingspan 40 inches; 3.5 pounds.
Diet: grains, insects, and small aquatic plants, mollusks and fish.
Sounds: a loud quack.

The mallard is easily recognized by its blue speculum (wing band) and, in the male, emerald-green head, white neck-band, and rusty-colored breast. The wide-ranging mallards are usually seen in the wild, dabbling and tipping in the shallows of fresh- and saltwater bodies, but they are not shy around humans and are often found waiting patiently for handouts around park ponds, waterfront cafes, and similar civilized habitat. In water they rarely dive; in flight they are agile and take off nearly vertically.

The tracks are typical of all waterfowl, as well as coastal birds including all seagulls, cormorants, terns, shearwaters, petrels, gannets, jaegers, and the alcids (razorbills, murres, dovekie, guillemots, and puffins). All these birds have hind toes so small and elevated that they do not leave imprints. The three main toes fan out in front and are connected by webs, which nearly always leave prints. Tracks like these will range in size from somewhat less than 2 inches long for small ducks to 7 inches for whistling swans. Once again, with tracks as initial clues, patient field work and an intimate knowledge of the species frequenting the area at the time of year the tracks are found will allow you to accurately guess the track maker's identity.

Mallard
life size in mud

GREAT HORNED OWL *Bubo virginianus*
Cat owl

Order: Strigiformes (owls). **Family:** Strigidae (owls). **Range and habitat:** widespread throughout California; from forests to deserts to mountain cliff faces. **Size and weight:** length 24 inches, wingspan 48 inches; 3.5 pounds. **Diet:** rabbits, mice, rats, voles, skunks, and grouse. **Sounds:** males normally hoot four or five times in sequence, females six to eight times.

This common, large, "eared" owl does look catlike when it sits staring at you from a lofty perch or nesting tree. The male and female prefer to use nests constructed in previous years by hawks or ravens rather than building their own, and they nest so early in spring that the brooding female is often partially covered with snow. Special modifications of its wing feathers allow this night hunter to drop silently onto the back of unsuspecting prey.

The shape of the tracks illustrated is representative of numerous species of California owls, including the screech, long-eared, short-eared, burrowing, saw-whet, and pygmy owls. Owl tracks are uncommon except in snow country, where an owl may leave a few tracks around a kill site or when it lands to investigate and feed on food too heavy to carry away. You may also find owl tracks on recently rained-upon dirt roads where an owl has discovered a car-killed animal.

The tracks of the great horned owl in mud show its three thick, powerful toes and imprints of its long, sharp talons. The hind toe mark is always insignificant or absent. Smaller owl species obviously leave smaller tracks. Unless you are lucky enough to see these smaller owls in the act of making tracks, there's no way to identify the tracks by species. You might get a clue by observing the area at dusk, the best time for sighting owls, to see what species are present in the vicinity of the tracks you have found.

Great Horned Owl
life size in mud

GREAT BLUE HERON *Ardea herodias*

Order: Ciconiiformes (herons and allies). **Family:** Ardeidae (herons, egrets, and bitterns). **Range and habitat:** widespread throughout California; in most lowland areas, common on freshwater and ocean shores. **Size and weight:** length 48 inches, wingspan 72 inches; 7 pounds. **Diet:** fish, snakes, insects, mice, and frogs. **Sounds:** "kraak" and strident honks.

The presence of a great blue heron magically transforms an aquatic landscape, adding an aura of quiet elegance characteristic of the best Oriental brush paintings. This large heron typically walks slowly through shallows or stands with head hunched on shoulders, looking for the fish that make up a large part of its diet. A heron's nest, maintained year after year, is an elaborate structure of sticks 3 feet across built in a tree; great blue herons often nest colonially.

You will most often find great blue heron tracks bordering the freshwater areas where the bird feeds. The four toes and claws of each foot usually leave visible imprints. The well-developed hind toe enables the heron to stand for long periods of time on one leg or the other or to walk very slowly while hunting.

This track shape is typical of all the herons, egrets, bitterns, cranes, rails, and American coot found in California. The size and location of the tracks will vary according to species.

Great Blue Heron
life size in mud

GOLDEN EAGLE *Aquila chrysaetos*

Order: Falconiformes (raptors). **Family:** Accipitridae (hawks, kites, and eagles). **Range and habitat:** year-round throughout California; in remote mountains, grasslands, and deserts. **Size and weight:** length 32 inches, wingspan more than 72 inches; 10 pounds. **Diet:** primarily rodents; occasionally other small mammals, birds, and fish. **Sounds:** rapid, sharp chips.

Both the adult and the immature golden eagle have a rich, dark brown body plumage; the golden neck feathers are visible only at close range. The broad white tail band and white wing patches of the immature bird are good field marks. These birds exhibit typical buteo flight, with very long rounded wings.

The golden eagle is rare and endangered; if you sight one or find its tracks, consider it a lucky day. The golden eagle's track shape—four equally prominent toe and claw imprints—is also representative of the turkey vulture, the osprey, and many species of hawks and falcons that are found within California. The size and location of the tracks will vary depending on the particular species.

Golden Eagle
life size in mud

Recommended Reading

CARE OF THE WILD FEATHERED AND FURRED: A Guide to Wildlife Handling and Care, Mae Hickman and Maxine Guy (Unity Press, 1973); unique perspectives on animal behavior and emergency care of injured and orphaned wildlife.

A FIELD GUIDE TO ANIMAL TRACKS, Olaus J. Murie (Houghton Mifflin Co., Boston, 2nd ed., 1975); a classic work on track identification by Murie (1889–1963), an eminent naturalist and wildlife artist; one of the Peterson Field Guide Series; an excellent research text for home study.

ISLAND SOJOURN, Elizabeth Arthur (Harper & Row, 1980); an account of life on an island in British Columbia's wilderness, with a chapter devoted to a metaphysical perspective of animal tracks.

SNOW TRACKS, Jean George (E. P. Dutton, 1958); an introduction to the study of animal tracks for very young children.

THE TRACKER, Tom Brown and William J. Watkins (Berkley Publications, 1984); an intriguing story by a man who has devoted his life to the science of following tracks and other movement clues of various animals, including humans.

Index

Alcids 116
Anas platyrhynchos 116
Antelope 84
Antilocapra americana 84
Aplodontia 48
Aplodontia rufa 48
Aquila chrysaetos 122
Ardea herodias 120
Badger 72
Bassariscus astutus 58
Bear, black 82, 106
Bear, grizzly 106
Beaver 104
Beaver, mountain 48
Beetles 12
Bighorn, desert 90
Bitterns 120
Boar, wild 88
Bobcat 66
Bubo virginianus 118
Bufo boreas 30
Bullfrog 64
Cacomistle 58
Canis latrans 70
Castor canadensis 104
Cat, civet 46, 58
Cat, domestic 66, 82
Cat, miner's 58
Catamount 94
Centipede 12
Cervus elaphus 92
Charadrius vociferus 112
Chickaree 34
Chipmunk, Allen's yellow-pine 20
Chipmunk, alpine 20
Chipmunk, least 20
Chipmunk, lodgepole 20
Chipmunk, long-eared 20

Chipmunk, Merriam's 20
Chipmunk, Panamint 20
Chipmunk, Sonora 20
Chipmunks 24
Cony 24
Coot, American 120
Cormorants 116
Corvus brachyrhynchos 114
Cottontail, desert 96
Cottontail, mountain 96
Cottontail, Nuttall's 96
Cottontails 68, 100
Cougar 94
Coyote 70, 100
Cranes 120
Cricket 12
Crow, American 114
Deer 84
Deer, mule 86, 88, 92
Deer, white-tailed 86
Didelphis virginiana 54
Dipodomys heermanni 26
Dog, domestic 70
Dovekie 116
Ducks 112, 116
Eagle, golden 122
Egrets 120
Elk 90, 92
Ermine 28
Eutamias speciosus 20
Falcons 122
Felis concolor 94
Felis rufus 66
Fisher 60, 74, 80
Flying squirrel, northern 38
Fox, gray 68
Frogs 64
Gannet 116

Geckos 32
Glaucomys sabrinus 38
Gophers, pocket 18
Ground squirrel, California 22, 36
Ground squirrel, golden-mantled 22
Guillemots 116
Gulls 112
Gulo gulo 82
Hare, snowshoe 98, 100
Hawks 114
Heron, great blue 120
Insects 12
Invertebrates 12
Jackrabbit, black-tailed 98
Jackrabbit, white-tailed 98
Jackrabbits 96, 98, 100
Jaegers 116
Junco hyemalis 110
Junco, northern 110
Kangaroo rat, desert 26
Kangaroo rat, Heermann's 26
Kangaroo rat, Merriam's 26
Killdeer 112
Lepus americanus 100
Lepus californicus 98
Lion, mountain 94
Lizards 32
Lutra canadensis 80
Lynx 66
Mallard 116
Marmot, yellow-bellied 56
Marmota flaviventris 56
Marten 44, 60, 74
Martes americana 60
Martes pennanti 74
Mephitis mephitis 62
Mice 14
Mink 44, 60
Mouse, brush 14
Mouse, cactus 14
Mouse, canyon 14

Mouse, deer 14
Mouse, grasshopper 14
Mouse, harvest 14
Mouse, house 14
Mouse, pinon 14
Mouse, pocket 14
Mouse, western 14
Mouse, white-footed 14
Murres 116
Muskrat 44, 50, 80
Mustela erminea 28
Mustela frenata 28
Mustela vison 44
Neotoma fuscipes 42
Ochotona princeps 24
Odocoileus hemionus 86
Ondatra zibethicus 50
Opossum, Virginia 54
Osprey 122
Otter, river 80
Ovis canadensis 90
Owl, burrowing 118
Owl, great horned 118
Owl, long-eared 118
Owl, pygmy 118
Owl, saw-whet 118
Owl, screech 118
Owl, short-eared 118
Owls 114
Panther 94
Peromyscus maniculatus 14
Petrels 116
Pig, domestic 88
Pika 24
Pocket gopher, Mazama 18
Pocket gopher, northern 18
Pocket gopher, Sierra 18
Pocket gopher, Townsend 18
Porcupine 72, 74, 76
Procyon lotor 78
Pronghorn 84

Puffins 116
Puma 94
Rabbit, brush 96
Rabbit, pygmy 96
Rabbits 96, 98, 100
Raccoon 56, 78
Rails 120
Rana catesbiana 64
Rat, black 42
Rat, brown 50
Rat, kangaroo 26
Rat, Norway 42
Rat, pack 42
Rats 18
Raven 118
Razorbill 116
Ringtail 58, 78
Sable, American 60
Sandpipers 112
Sciurus griseus 52
Seagulls 116
Shearwaters 116
Sheep, bighorn 90
Sheep, mountain 90
Shorebirds 112
Shrew, dusky 16
Shrews 14
Skunk 44, 46
Skunk, spotted 46, 58, 62
Skunk, striped 46, 62
Snakes 40
Sorex obscurus 16
Spermophilus beecheyi 36
Spermophilus lateralis 22
Spilogale gracilis 46
Squamata 40
Squirrel, Douglas' 34, 60
Squirrel, flying 38

Squirrel, western gray 52
Squirrels, ground 22, 24, 48
Sus scrofa 88
Swan, whistling 116
Sylvilagus nuttalli 96
Tamiasciurus douglasii 34
Taxidea taxus 72
Terns 116
Testudines 102
Thomomys bottae 18
Toad, red-spotted 30
Toad, western 30
Tortoise, desert 102
Turtle, green 102
Turtle, hawksbill 102
Turtle, leatherback 102
Turtle, loggerhead 102
Turtles 102, 104
Urocyon cinereoargenteus 68
Ursus americanus 106
Voles 14
Vulture, turkey 122
Wapiti 92
Waterfowl 116
Weasel 28, 44, 74, 80, 82
Weasel, long-tailed 28, 44
Weasel, short-tailed 28
Whistler 56
Wildcat 66
Wolf, brush 70
Wolf, gray 70
Wolf, prairie 70
Wolverine 82
Woodrat, bushy-tailed 42
Woodrat, desert 42
Woodrat, dusky-footed 42
Yellowlegs, greater 112

About the author:

Chris Stall first became interested in wild country and wild animals during several years with a very active Boy Scout troop in rural New York State, where he spent his youth. In the two decades since then he has travelled and lived around most of North America, studying, photographing, sketching and writing about wild animals in their natural habitats. His photos and articles have appeared in a number of outdoor and nature magazines. Stall currently lives in Cincinnati, his launching point for a 1365-mile solo kayak journey down the Mississippi River to New Orleans in 1988.